Karma
A Spiritual and Scientific Perspective

Unlock the secrets of Karma and transform your life.

Author: Chavda Mukeshbhai Kalabhai

Writing Collaborator: Chavda Jyotiben Mukeshbhai

ISBN: 978-93-343-0638-5

(Paperback / softback)

Book Ready Date: May 20, 2025

This book was written by: **Chavda Mukeshbhai Kalabhai.**

Writing Collaborator: **Chavda Jyoti Mukeshbhai**

Email: **chavda206706@gmail.com**

Disclaimer

The views and information expressed in this book are based on the author's personal experiences, research, and spiritual understanding. This information is provided for educational and inspirational purposes only. It should not be considered a substitute for professional advice, such as medical, psychological, legal, or financial guidance.

The author and publisher do not accept any responsibility for any direct or indirect consequences arising from the use or misuse of the content in this book. Readers are advised to seek qualified professional advice pertaining to their specific circumstances.

Dedication

I dedicate this book to my beloved family, who have always filled my life with love, support, and meaning.

To my respected father, Shri Kalabhai Maldehbhai Chavada, and my late mother, Smt. Maluben Kalabhai Chavada — whose teachings, blessings, and memories continue to empower me on my spiritual journey.

To my life partner, Jyoti, who has been my fellow traveler and inspiration on this path.

To my younger brother, Kishore, and his wife, Artiben, who are an integral part of our family and always provide me with companionship and loving support.

To my five dear children — Yug, Bhoomi (my son and daughter), and Rimen, Trisha, Akshara (my brother Kishore's children) — whose smiles and love light up my life. Our home is full of love and harmony, and this book is a symbol of our deep relationships and shared values.

My gratitude to the teachers, books, and guides who have helped me understand the mysteries of Karma, the soul, and life.

Special Thanks To Shri Mahendra Chaturbhuj, who has been my friend since school time and my guru on the path of meditation. Under his invaluable guidance, the regular practice of Sri Sri Ravi Shankarji's Sudarshan Kriya and other meditation practices has proven immensely beneficial for my life. And finally, thanks to all the readers who have joined me on this journey through this book. This journey would not have been possible without all of you. **Thank you.**

Table of Contents

Chapters Page No.

Your karma is destiny's blueprint!

Sow goodness, and guarantee yourself a sweet life ahead.

Introduction

Yes, friends, understanding the depths of Karma and performing the right actions is vital in life. You've probably wondered many times how much our actions can influence our future. Should we truly always do good deeds? Does the harm from wrong actions only affect us, or does it impact the world too? Does anything remain after life ends? If so, what is it, and what role do our actions play in it? Is this world truly as we perceive it?

My name is **Chavda Mukesh**. I live in a small town near Rajkot, Gujarat. Since childhood, many profound questions have arisen in my mind: Does the soul truly exist? Is reincarnation real? If so, how does it work? Is there a God, or are they just a concept? Is there someone watching our good and bad deeds? Do our actions affect this world, the universe, or our soul? Are our souls and rebirth truly bound by our actions? These weren't just curious questions for me; they became the foundation of my life's direction and way of thinking.

On this journey of faith and science, my wife, Jyoti, has been more than just my companion; as a fellow traveler, she's often inspired me to think from new perspectives.

Her collaboration, support, and ideas have played a significant role in making this book more complete. Without her, this work wouldn't have been possible, and for that, I express my heartfelt gratitude.

During this writing journey, there were many times I felt as an unknown inspiration was guiding my thoughts—as if some ideas were transmitted to me telepathically.

There was a time when I was a complete atheist. I believed that everything was limited to this life only. "If we exist, this world exists. If we don't, nothing does." I used to think that my

relationships, my identity, and my actions existed only as long as I was alive. After death, everything would end—neither I nor my actions would remain; everything would vanish with time. And I know many people still think this way today. These very thoughts and the quest to explore them became an integral part of my life. But time introduced me to new experiences and amazing truths.

As I tried to understand the deeper mysteries of the soul, reincarnation, and karma, my thinking gradually began to change.

Chapter 01. Is Anyone Observing Our Karma?

Time passed, and as my search progressed, I realized that this world is not as we perceive it. Behind it exists an unknown power, a highly intelligent system, or perhaps a higher level of energy, that keeps this entire universe in balance. It cannot be a mere coincidence that everything operates according to its own rules. Every living being, every element, every process functions under an unseen plan.

For example:

Balance in Nature: In the jungle, it has never happened that only lions remained and deer disappeared. Every species maintains its limited population, which keeps nature balanced.

Complex Design of the Human Body: Our respiratory system, digestive system, heart, brain—everything functions with such complexity and precision that it cannot be mere coincidence. Our skin heals automatically when cut, our cells regenerate themselves, and our bones strengthen over time.

Natural Cycles: We take in oxygen, while plants take in carbon dioxide and, in return, give us oxygen. This is a cycle balanced by some unseen intelligence.

Seed and Life: A tiny seed transforms into a massive tree, which then produces thousands of seeds that give rise to more trees. Every fruit contains seeds that have the ability to replicate their own form and contribute greatly to maintaining nature's balance.

Precise Balance of Planets: Think about how many unseen forces are at work to keep Earth stable. If oxygen suddenly disappeared from Earth, life would end in mere seconds. If the sun suddenly vanished, Earth would turn into ice due to darkness and cold. If the distance between Earth and the sun increased or decreased

even slightly, life would become impossible.

Protection of Earth: Just as the giant planet Jupiter, with its powerful gravitational force, pulls large meteoroids (asteroids) towards itself from space, it acts like an invisible shield for us and has consistently protected Earth.

There are so many such examples that if I were to write them all here, the book would be filled with just those.

When everything in the universe operates with such balance, planning, and precision, how can it be possible that our actions are meaningless and that no one observes them? When every law of nature is bound by a deep order—the rising and setting of the sun, the Earth rotating on its axis, the cycle of life and death for every living being—how can our actions be separate from this system? Do not be under any misconception; our actions are a very important part of this universe. Whatever we think, say, and do is being recorded somewhere, and its results return with the same precision with which this universe operates. This is why understanding karma and guiding it in the right direction is our most important task.

On this journey, I have deeply understood and realized many aspects of how the cycle of karma affects our lives. Everyone's life reaches a point when they must reflect on their actions, whether what they did was right or wrong. Karma is not just a theory; it is the fundamental truth of our lives, shaping our existence every moment. Whatever we do, we receive its consequences. If not today, then tomorrow. If not in this life, then in the next. This is why choosing the right actions is so crucial.

This book is not merely a collection of my thoughts. It is a compilation of experiences, events, and evidence that I have seen and heard on my journey. In it, I have shared lessons from my life and those facts (proof) that convince me that the principle of karma is not just a spiritual idea but a scientific truth. In this book, I have tried to present you with evidence of the truth of karma—whether that evidence comes from other books or from renowned experiments and research. I have also shared references to some documentaries that will help in understanding this subject in depth.

In this book, you will learn how our actions shape us. How the impact of every small and large action affects not only our current life but also our future lives. You will also understand the importance of performing right actions and how wrong actions can weaken and confuse our soul.

This is not just a book; it is an effort to understand and improve your life. So, friends, let's embark on this journey together. In it, you will find answers to questions, exploration into the depths of the soul, and an attempt to understand the meaning of life.

Remember, only one thing is permanent in this world—our karma. Nothing goes with us except our actions. This is our true wealth. This is our identity. Whenever we take a new birth, whatever our form in that life, we learn something new. Every life gives us another opportunity to better ourselves. This is the very purpose of the Supreme Father, the Supreme Soul, for us: that we become good, kind, and filled with love. Each time, each birth brings us closer to this goal of recognizing the compassion and love within us and manifesting it in the world through our actions.

Many times in life, we are surrounded by difficulties and think—"Why is this happening to me?" In this book, you will find answers to those questions. You will understand that every suffering, every struggle, is not a punishment, but a test for the soul that strengthens us and brings us closer to our true self.

Remember, when this body turns to dust, when wealth, relationships, and connections are left behind, what will go with you is what is truly yours—your karma. Those very actions will welcome you in the next birth; they will give you a new direction. Therefore, the seeds we sow today will become the fruits in our life tomorrow.

As you turn the pages of this book, you will find that these are not just tales of the past. This is connected to your present and will shape your coming future. You will learn how every day, every moment gives us the opportunity to improve our actions, purify our soul, and take one more step towards that ultimate truth.

Chapter 02. Connection of Karma and Life

Have you ever considered that after attaining supreme knowledge, great personalities always paid special attention to their actions and consistently kept them good and pure? Some of these great personalities include:

- **Gautam Buddha** – The founder of Buddhism, who attained Nirvana through meditation.
- **Osho (Rajneesh)** – A prominent advocate of modern meditation and spirituality.
- **Lao Tzu** – The founder of Taoism, whose teachings were based on meditation and harmony with nature.
- **Mahavir Swami** – The proponent of Jainism, who centered his teachings on meditation and non-violence.
- **Maharishi Patanjali** – The author of the Yoga Sutras, who clarified the principles of meditation and Yoga.
- **Krishna** – The great personality who taught meditation and Karma Yoga in the Bhagavad Gita.
- R**amakrishna Paramahamsa** – An Indian saint who experienced the soul through meditation and Bhakti Yoga.
- **Thi**ch **Nhat Hanh** – A Vietnamese Buddhist monk who made meditation and mindfulness a part of life.
- **Sant Kabir** – A saint of the Bhakti movement who sought truth through meditation and spiritual practice.
- **Swami Vivekananda** – An Indian saint who presented the importance of meditation and Yoga on a global stage.
- **Nikola Tesla** – A great scientist who used meditation and mental concentration for his creativity and profound insights.

Countless such great personalities have been born on this Earth and will continue to be, guiding humanity with their lives. If you observe carefully, you will find a deep commonality among all these luminaries: self-reflection, meditation, and benevolent actions. When a person sincerely embarks on self-realization and the search for truth, they ultimately realize that the fundamental basis of life is to always keep their actions pure, righteous, and virtuous. This is the secret that not only makes life successful but also fills the soul with deep contentment and divine joy.

The real story of your life begins the moment you take your first step into this world. With birth, one thing becomes certain: you have to perform actions. Whatever you do, or even if you do nothing, action is involved in every situation. If you decide not to perform a task, that too is an action. And if injustice is happening before your eyes, and you can stop it but remain silent, then you also become a part of that wrongful action.

Karma isn't just what we do; it's also what we don't do when we should have.

I've shared this incident from the Mahabharata as an example, but this book isn't written about any one religion, sect, or specific deity. It's for all of humanity. The principle of karma isn't limited to a single culture or tradition; it's an eternal law of the entire universe. **My aim isn't to promote any religion** but to bring forth the truth of karma, so that every individual can choose the right actions in their life and build a better society and world.

In the Mahabharata war, Lord Krishna had vowed that he would not pick up any weapon or strike anyone in battle. But when Bhishma Pitamah wreaked havoc on the Pandavas from the Kauravas' side and Arjuna failed to stop him, Krishna broke his vow. He leaped from his chariot, picked up a chariot wheel in his hand, and, burning with rage, advanced towards Bhishma

Pitamah.

Seeing this sight, Bhishma Pitamah stood firm in his place. There was astonishment on his face. He was overwhelmed by Krishna's divine play. He said, "O Madhav! You had promised that you would not pick up arms in battle and would not strike anyone, then why did you break your vow? Was my offense so great that Lord Krishna himself had to break his vow? Please tell me if I have committed any unrighteousness. I did what was in the best interest of Hastinapura, because I have vowed to serve Hastinapura as long as I live."

Krishna's face glowed with anger. In his eyes, there was both affection and sternness simultaneously. He roared in anger, "O Ganga-putra Bhishma! If upholding a vow means supporting injustice, then it is right to break such a vow at that very moment. When Draupadi was disrobed, you remained silent due to your vow. When the Kauravas consistently followed unrighteousness, you still remained silent. Is this the nature of Dharma, to let unrighteousness run rampant?"

Then Krishna calmed down a little and, showing compassion towards Bhishma, continued, "O Ganga-putra Bhishma, you are upholding your vow, but is Hastinapura benefiting? Don't you see that this war is happening within your own family, between your own grandsons? In the flow of time, you haven't even realized when your vow went against public welfare! Today, due to you, a massacre of your family and thousands of others is about to take place here! If you had wished, this war wouldn't have happened. You were so powerful that you could have stopped it. Yes, for that, you would have had to go against Duryodhana and Dhritarashtra, but would that truly have been wrong? Wouldn't it have been right for you to stand on the side of justice and righteousness to stop injustice and unrighteousness? Was your duty merely to uphold a vow? Was it not your duty to protect Dharma for the welfare of the people?"

Then Krishna paused for a few moments and, calming his anger slightly, said, "If I break my vow today, what's the worst that can happen? People will misunderstand me, they will accuse me, but I find it more appropriate to break my vow than to commit a wrong action. If I have to pay any price to stop this unrighteousness, if the whole world misunderstands me, I will gladly accept it."

Krishna's words shook Bhishma Pitamah's heart. He deeply realized his mistake. Scenes of his past sins and blunders flooded before his eyes—the injustice done to Amba, remaining silent during Draupadi's disrobing, supporting Duryodhana's atrocities, and his inability to speak against Dhritarashtra's biased policies. Tears of repentance welled up in his eyes. The bow slipped from his hands, as if the very roots of his resolve had been shaken. His weapons fell from his hands, and he prostrated himself at Lord Krishna's feet. After this incident, he decided to withdraw from the war and end his life.

That warrior, who had upheld his vow throughout his life, was now understanding for the first time that Dharma lies not merely in rules, but in duty and justice.

Chapter 03. Benefits of Righteous Karma

I know, friends, that no matter how determined we are not to perform wrong actions, life constantly brings us to crossroads where it seems there's no option but to do something wrong. Such situations often confuse us, making wrongful actions seem unavoidable.

But based on my experience and the insights gained on this journey, I'd tell you to control your mind as much as possible and try your best to avoid all types of wrongful actions. Whatever you do, do it in a state of complete awareness. What I mean is, while performing an action, you should at least know whether you're doing right or wrong and what your future will become as a result of that action.

No matter how difficult the circumstances, it's always possible to avoid wrongful actions. This depends on how strong your resolve is regarding your actions. We must rely on our discernment and patience. Try to walk the right path as much as possible, because the outcome of every action is certain.

In this chapter, we'll discuss the effects of right and wrong actions. So, let's first understand the unique benefits of right actions and how they can positively transform our lives.

Right actions, whether small or big, leave a positive impact on our lives. They bring us mental peace, self-respect, and contentment. Doing the right thing not only purifies our inner energy but also creates a positive atmosphere around us. When we perform right actions, we feel an amazing sense of self-confidence and tranquility within, which is more valuable than any material comfort. The greatest benefit of right actions is that they steer our cycle of karma in a positive direction. This cycle of karma continues endlessly, and right actions show us the way forward in life. Walking the right path opens doors of opportunity for us and makes it easier to achieve our goals.

So, in this chapter, we'll discuss the invaluable benefits of right actions in detail and learn how doing the right thing can improve our lives.

Perhaps you're thinking that we all already know about the benefits of right actions – they bring peace of mind, make us feel good, increase the joy of living, and leave no burden on our heart. Right? Didn't I say it right? But believe me, friends, the benefits of right actions aren't limited to just these. There's much more that we often overlook or aren't even aware of.

Right actions don't just give us peace of mind and self-satisfaction; they also offer an opportunity to elevate our entire life and personality to a new height. Through right actions, we can bring positivity and inspiration into the lives of those around us. This brings about deep internal transformation, making us feel proud of ourselves and strengthening our soul. So, let's embark on this journey to understand the amazing and profound benefits of right actions that fill our lives with new meaning and purpose.

Let's consider some important benefits of right actions:

Physical Well-being: Right actions keep the body healthy and help prevent many diseases.

Peace in the Family: Happiness and peace prevail at home; conflicts are avoided. Mutual love and cooperation among family members increase.

Progress in Work: Work and business prosper, and the path to success becomes easier.

Spiritual Strength: Right actions make our soul strong and powerful, filling us with confidence and courage.

Absolution from Past Sins: The burden of our past life sins is reduced, allowing us to experience a peaceful life.

Aura: Right actions brighten our aura, making our personality, confidence, and outlook more appealing.

Physical Well-being:

Right actions keep the body healthy and help prevent many diseases.

When we perform right actions, our mind remains calm and our soul happy, which also has a positive effect on the body. Right actions not only maintain our mental balance but also serve as a means of preventing illnesses.

You might have noticed that when someone experiences a heart attack, high blood pressure, or stress-related problems, doctors often ask – "Are you feeling tension? Do you have any kind of mental pressure?" Such questions directly indicate that mental and physical health are interconnected. The burden of wrong actions puts heavy pressure on our minds. Losses in business, family discord, debt, or regret over our own mistakes weaken us from within, and this guilt also affects our physical health.

Our body and soul are deeply connected. When we perform wrong actions, we think no one is watching, but nothing is hidden from our soul. Our soul is always a witness to our actions. Every wrong deed grieves our soul, and this sorrow manifests in our body as diseases. This is why many serious illnesses such as heart disease, diabetes, depression, digestive problems, headaches, migraines, and insomnia enter our lives.

Friends, have you ever noticed that everything in nature maintains a beautiful balance? God, or rather, nature, maintains harmony in this world in every way. Whether it's the population of living beings or the distribution of resources, everything remains balanced in its own way. If we observe carefully, nature periodically re-establishes balance according to its rules. This natural order sustains this creation, and we see countless proofs of it all around us.

Similarly, nature also maintains the balance of evil. Whenever an evil force emerges, a good force is born in some form or another to neutralize it. This natural law also applies to our actions. If we continuously perform wrong actions, we inevitably have to face their consequences. Our life is, in a way, a mirror of nature – we reap what we sow. This balance teaches us that no matter how great the evil we face, goodness is also with us. And in this way, we should focus on our actions to maintain this balance and stay on the right path.

Peace in the Family:

Happiness and peace prevail at home, arguments don't happen, and mutual love and cooperation among family members increase.

When the head of a family is true to their actions, honest, and follows the right path in life—then happiness and prosperity naturally flow into that home. The energy of their inner truth gradually illuminates the entire family. Their every action is one that benefits others, and the wealth earned from it also brings good energy. This positive energy deeply settles into the food, the atmosphere, and the children's values in that home. Such wealth nourishes the body and satisfies the mind. Even if the earned wealth isn't in large amounts, there is contentment in the mind, and a good, deep sleep comes at night.

A person who consistently performs right actions develops a special kind of peace of mind. This peace becomes so precious that the person resolves firmly within—that they will not disturb that peace under any circumstances. They clearly experience that if they were to stray onto a wrong path, this inner peace could be lost. And once a person truly tastes the genuine flavor of peace of mind, they never wish to deviate from the path of right actions throughout their life.

The energy of right actions, though invisible, is extremely powerful. This energy not only increases love and cooperation within the family but also opens the way for progress in the life of every household member. When people in the home are engaged in good thoughts and good deeds, every day becomes a festival of joy there. Small moments are filled with love and belonging, and the home's atmosphere becomes as sacred as a pilgrimage site.

That's why it's said that right actions are the true capital of life. These actions strengthen the foundation of our homes, sweeten relationships, and raise children under the shadow of good values. When the tradition of right actions continues in a family, its happiness and prosperity flourish from generation to generation.

Families filled with happiness and peace have some invaluable habits that increase their good fortune from generation to generation. In such homes, family members eat meals together daily—because eating together not only nourishes the body but also connects the mind with love. Before meals, they remember their ancestors and express gratitude to God. This small habit maintains the flow of spiritual energy in their home.

These families have another beautiful characteristic—they always keep their minds clean and pure towards each other. If there is ever any disagreement or minor quarrel, they lovingly forgive each other. The feeling that "relationships shouldn't break; the dirt of the mind should be washed away in time" is deeply ingrained in their hearts. This is why their relationships grow stronger day by day, and peace and happiness prevail in the home.

The truth is, great joys are hidden in these small habits. When every family member respects these traditions, their home becomes a pilgrimage site where the stream of love, respect, and joy flows eternally. These very habits sow the seeds of prosperity and progress in the home, which the entire family sees flourish over time.

Just as we don't see electricity in electrical wires, but it's present, and we feel its effect. Similarly, the energy of wrong and right actions is invisible, but their results are clearly visible in our lives.

Now, let's look at some experiments to understand the effect of this energy. You can even try them yourself if you wish.

Experiment 1: Effect of Positive & Negative Communication

Place two plants in one spot. Every day, speak positive words to the first plant, such as "You are very good, I like you a lot, you will grow quickly and stay healthy." At the same time, say negative things to the second plant, such as "You are not good, I don't like you at all, you will wither quickly." In just a few weeks, you'll observe that the first plant becomes healthy and large, while the second plant begins to wilt.

Experiment 2: The Impact of Thoughts on Water

The credit for making the theory of human emotions and thoughts influencing water's structure world-renowned goes to Dr. Masaru Emoto.

In another experiment, some people practice positive and negative thoughts with two glasses of water. Take water in one glass and repeatedly speak positive words to it, such as "love, joy, happiness," etc. In the second glass, speak negative words such as "hate, sorrow, anger." After some time, when the water crystals from both glasses are examined under a microscope, the crystals from the water with positive words are beautiful and organized, whereas the crystals from the water with negative words are scattered and disorganized.

These experiments prove that the energy of our thoughts and actions affects not only our lives but also everything around us. When we perform wrong actions, we unknowingly attract negative energy into our lives, and its effect is also visible in the peace of our home. Conversely, performing right actions circulates positive energy into our lives and home-family, which increases mental peace and love in relationships.

Therefore, the importance of right actions isn't just in our external lives but also in our mental and spiritual health.

Progress in Work:

Work and business prosper, and the path to success becomes

easier.

The place where we work—be it an office, a shop, or our home—forms an **energy field**. This energy field repeatedly encourages you to do the same work. If you regularly sit in your spot and work with honesty, diligence, and dedication, that place makes you and others who come there feel pure, spiritually peaceful, and effective. The mind naturally begins to calm down there, and you feel a strange, yet good, sensation.

For example, you've probably noticed that when we go to a temple or a peaceful place, we experience a different kind of tranquility, as if the energy of that place soothes us. Conversely, in some places, we instinctively feel uneasy or anxious. This is the effect of the specific place's energy. Similarly, if you engage in wrongful acts at your office or shop, such as drinking alcohol, gambling, or plotting conspiracies, negative energy builds up there. Then, you won't find spiritual peace in that place, and others who come there also won't feel good. This impacts your work, trade, or business, and gradually, the business starts to decline, while income also decreases or is disrupted.

All of this happens, and we often don't understand why. Therefore, it's essential that we perform **right actions** to keep the energy of our workplace positive and create a healthy environment.

Spiritual Strength:

Right actions make our soul strong and powerful, filling us with confidence and courage.

Perhaps many of you won't believe that we even have a soul. But if you search on the internet, you'll find much evidence for this. I often suggest searching online because in today's modern world, everyone is connected to the internet, and a lot of information from various countries is available through it.

Our actions are connected to us and are also related to our many births. At every stage of life, our actions play a significant role in the development of our soul and its progression towards a higher state. Through right actions, we can purify our soul and strive to elevate it to a higher level.

When we perform right actions, it aids in our soul's evolution, allowing us to gain even more knowledge and experience in the next stage of life. This cycle of rebirth continues until our soul reaches a state of perfection (moksha).

In this process, following right actions not only leads our soul towards progress but also absolves the sins of our past lives. This is a golden opportunity to eliminate the negative energy accumulated in our soul and attract positive energy.

Conversely, following wrong actions leads to many disadvantages. When we perform wrong actions, we unknowingly attract negative energy into our lives, and its effect is also felt in the peace of our home. Performing right actions, on the other hand, circulates positive energy and peace between us and our home-family. This not only gives us mental peace but also increases love and understanding in our relationships.

Therefore, the importance of right actions is not just in our external lives but also in our mental and spiritual health. We should always strive to direct our actions in the right way. Right actions not only provide us with peace and contentment in this life but also propel our soul towards a higher journey. We are reborn repeatedly so that, through right actions, we can elevate our soul to a higher state.

Evidence for the Existence of the Soul:

If you doubt whether we even have a soul, let me try to provide you with some evidence.

Evidence 1: Out-of-Body Experiences During Meditation

You might have heard that people who practice meditation regularly sometimes experience being outside their body, with their subtle body connected to their physical body by a silver cord. This isn't imagination; when one goes deep into meditation, this experience can happen to anyone. Many spiritual seekers and yogis have directly experienced this.

Evidence 2: Near-Death Experiences (NDEs) and Out-of-Body Experiences (OBEs)

In hospitals, when a person is unconscious during an operation, or when someone is declared clinically dead for a few moments and then revives, they often recount Near-Death Experiences (NDEs) and Out-of-Body Experiences (OBEs). They describe seeing their body from outside, witnessing a tunnel of light, having divine experiences, and sometimes even meeting deceased relatives. Thousands of people have shared these experiences, and remarkable similarities have been found among them.

Evidence 3: Children's Past-Life Memories

Not just in India, but thousands of authenticated cases have been recorded worldwide where young children remember details from their previous lives. They vividly describe their past-life parents, home, village, and even the cause of their death—and when the veracity of their statements is investigated, they prove to be absolutely true.

Dr. Ian Stevenson, a renowned American psychologist, scientifically studied over 2,000 such cases globally. His research concluded that the existence of the soul is a reality. The most famous case in India is that of a girl named Shanti Devi, who, after being born in Delhi, recognized her past-life husband, home, street, and relatives in Mathura without ever having seen them before. This case was found to be completely true by several news agencies and judicial inquiries at the time.

Absolution from Past Sins:

The burden of our past-life sins is reduced, allowing us to experience a peaceful life.

Even after knowing all this, you might still wonder if things like **sin (paap)** and **virtue (punya)** truly exist. Is it all just an idea, or does it have a real existence? Now that we've considered evidence for the existence of the soul, reincarnation, and past lives, the question naturally arises: Is there such a thing as real sin and virtue? Is it merely a religious concept, or does it have a deeper, actual foundation?

Think seriously for a moment.

We take birth repeatedly in life. Is this just a coincidence? No. The continuous journey of our soul and the recurrence of actions indicate that this life is not a coincidence, but a well-planned process.

We are not merely a body of flesh and bones; within us is the divine essence of the **soul** that is conscious, aware, and experiences actions. This soul makes us realize that whatever we do, its effect isn't limited to the external world; it also influences our inner self and future lives.

Akashic Records: The Cosmic Ledger

Spiritual traditions mention the **Akashic Records**, which are referred to as the conscious repository of the universe. This is a divine archive where the minutest details of every thought, emotion, and action of our soul are recorded—whether they are good deeds or bad.

When we commit a sin, its **vibration** is registered in the universe. When we perform a virtuous act, its positive energy is also accumulated in this cosmic system. This is not just religious imagination but a truth gained through deep spiritual experience and practice.

Consider your own experiences.

Have you ever done something you still regret remembering? Have you ever said something that makes you feel sad to recall? That inner voice, that self-reproach—all of this is proof that sin and virtue are not just words, but a part of our spiritual experiences.

The Importance of Right Action

Regardless of what our past life actions may have been, in our current life, we can determine the direction of our future every moment. Every right action is like a lamp that not only illuminates the present but also diminishes the shadows of the past.

Right action is a stepping stone to **spiritual progress**. It not only makes our current life peaceful, prosperous, and balanced, but it also refines the quality of our future births.

Conclusion

Sin and virtue are not fabricated notions but are the basis for the subtle reckoning of actions. Soul, karma, and rebirth—these three are eternal truths of life that are deeply interconnected.

When we accept that the outcome of our actions is certain, we become aware. Then, every thought, every word, and every action of ours becomes purer, calmer, and more virtuous.

Therefore, consider every action an opportunity—to purify the soul, to improve life, and to move one step closer to that ultimate truth.

Aura:

Right actions brighten our aura, making our personality, confidence, and outlook more appealing.

One significant benefit of performing right actions is that our aura and positivity increase. An aura is an invisible energy field that surrounds every person. It's a reflection of our emotions, thoughts, and health status. From a scientific perspective, the aura is a combination of electrical and magnetic fields that indicates our emotional and mental well-being.

A happy and balanced person's aura is bright and colorful, whereas a stressed person's aura is dull and made up of negative colors. When we perform right actions, our energy is refined, which creates a positive aura. This not only keeps us balanced but also has a positive impact on others.

Right actions strengthen our soul, allowing us to easily overcome stress and negativity. This keeps our thoughts clear and our mind light, making us experience new energy and enthusiasm every day. A positive aura motivates us to achieve our goals and brings harmony to relationships.

So friends, try to perform right actions every day. Its effect is not just on the present life but also has a deep impact on the future. The continuous practice of right actions elevates our soul and creates a positive environment around us, benefiting us and our loved ones.

Science and the Aura

The scientific study of the aura became particularly popular in the 20th century. Semyon Kirlian, the father of Kirlian photography in Russia, claimed to have taken the first electrical image of the aura in 1939. He found that a faint halo of energy exists around every object and living being. He called this "radiant emission," which we know today as the aura.

Science has viewed it as a "bioelectric field" or "energy field." Many scientists believe that the aura indicates our health and mental state. For example:

Hans Berger, through his Electroencephalogram (EEG) experiments, showed that the brain's electrical activities influence our aura.

The California Institute of Integral Studies has developed instruments to measure and understand the aura.

Several institutions in Japan have conducted research on energy healing and the aura.

Experiments Enhancing Aura's Energy

These experiments show that our mental and emotional state has a profound impact on our aura. When we perform positive actions, meditate, or channelize inspiration and the soul's energy in the right direction, our aura is enhanced.

Kirlian Photography: Using this technique, scientists have recorded changes in the colors and shapes of the aura under different emotions and conditions.

Biofield Research: This research indicates that positive actions and meditation make the aura balanced and bright.

Influence of Inspiration and Soul: Research also shows that right actions improve mental balance and the power of the aura.

Connection Between Aura and Your Life

When we perform right actions, our aura naturally becomes bright and balanced. This not only keeps our energy at a high level but also has a positive effect on those around us. Scientists have found that a positive aura also inspires others.

Benefits of an Aura Formed by Right Actions

Improved Health: A positive aura improves mental and physical health. It reduces stress and fatigue.

Harmony in Relationships: A bright aura strengthens our relationships with others.

Increased Self-Confidence: The enhancement of the aura makes our personality attractive and empowers our soul.

To Understand This More Deeply

If you wish to know more about the aura or seek further evidence, you can research these topics: "**Kirlian Photography**" and related research. Published studies on "**Biofield Science**" and "Energy Healing."

Search on the internet for "**Aura Scanning Institutes**" and "**Energy Field Photography**."

You might find useful material on reliable websites like PubMed, ResearchGate, and Spiritual Science Foundation. You can also find information about institutions using Kirlian photography-related images and devices.

The enhancement of the aura is not just a scientific or spiritual process. It's a way of living life. A life filled with right actions, truth, and kindness can make your aura bright and powerful.

Friends, remember! Right actions can change not just your aura, but your entire world.

Chapter 04. Harms of Wrongful Karma

Life. Our actions hold immense importance. Good deeds bring us happiness and positivity, while wrong actions lead to many problems in life. The impact of wrongful actions isn't just on our mental and physical health but also on our relationships and financial situation.

Negative Effects of Wrongful Karma:

- Spiritual damage
- Impact on physical health
- Discord in the family and strained relationships
- Financial losses
- Mental burden
- Lack of positivity

Spiritual Damage:

Wrong actions deeply affect our soul. When we engage in unethical or improper acts, a kind of impurity settles upon our soul. This impurity disrupts our inner peace, leaving us feeling restless and discontent. Our mental health is impacted in this process, and this dissatisfaction begins to show in every aspect of life. People often think that nothing goes with us after death. But this notion is entirely false. The truth is that after death, our soul embarks on a journey with its accumulated karma. Think of it like the energy of our actions remaining connected to us, just as money deposited in a bank account stays with us. Our actions, whether good or bad, create our "karma account." These accounts determine the direction of our soul and its future experiences.

It's essential to understand that this life is merely one

chapter; the soul's journey is much longer and deeper than that. With each birth, the soul accumulates new experiences and lessons. Whatever we learn or do in this life becomes a part of our soul's energy and nature. This is reflected in our habits, temperament, and character. To grasp this process, life can be seen as a vast school. Each birth is a new class, and its purpose is to guide the soul towards perfection.

According to ancient scriptures and modern spiritual thought, our journey isn't limited to Earth. The soul may have to travel to many other dimensions and realms to gain more experience and knowledge. As the soul learns from its actions, it strives to become better in every birth. Good actions elevate the soul to a higher level, while bad actions can push it in a negative direction. This can be understood like a student's performance being crucial for their entry into the next grade.

When we understand that our life isn't merely limited to material pleasures but is a means for the soul's purification and progress, we become more aware of our actions. The greatest benefit of good actions is that they purify and elevate our soul. Conversely, wrong actions contaminate the soul. This contamination isn't limited to this life; its impact continues into subsequent births.

The purpose of life isn't merely to attain worldly pleasures but to guide the soul towards perfection. Every action holds significance in this journey of the soul. Our actions not only affect our current life but also profoundly impact our soul's entire journey. Therefore, it's essential that we perform our actions with wisdom and responsibility. Only through righteous actions can we fill our "karma account" with positive energy and elevate the soul to higher dimensions.

The damage caused to the soul by wrong actions reminds us that every moment of life is valuable. This isn't just a one-time opportunity but a continuous journey. This journey is one of the soul's progress and purification, and every action can either help or hinder us in achieving it.

Impact on physical health:

Wrong actions can also take a toll on our bodies. As we get entangled in negative behaviors, **stress and anxiety** tend to increase, which can lead to problems like **high blood pressure, heart disease, and depression**. Research shows that prolonged stress can weaken our immune system, making us more vulnerable to various illnesses.

Health Issues Caused by Stress

Being under constant tension negatively affects the body and can lead to several physical and mental health problems. Here are some of the main conditions linked to stress:

- **Heart Disease:** Long-term stress puts excessive strain on the heart, potentially raising blood pressure and increasing the risk of heart attacks. Persistent tension can be very damaging to heart health.
- **Diabetes:** Stress can disrupt insulin levels in the body. During stressful periods, blood sugar tends to rise, which can increase the risk of developing diabetes.
- **Depression and Anxiety:** Extended periods of tension can worsen feelings of hopelessness, sadness, and restlessness. This severely impacts mental well-being and can trigger depression.
- **Digestive Problems:** Stress has a direct effect on our digestive system. It can cause issues like acidity, gas, stomach pain, and constipation. Severe tension can even

lead to inflammation in the intestines.

- **Headaches and Migraines:** Stress frequently causes headaches or migraine problems, which can become more severe when a person is constantly under pressure.
- **Weak Immune System:** Tension can weaken the body's immune system, making individuals more prone to frequent illnesses and susceptible to infections.
- **Joint and Muscle Pain:** Stress often causes muscles and nerves in the body to tense up, leading to pain in bones and muscles. If this condition persists, it can even contribute to problems like arthritis.
- **Sleep Disorders:** Stress can cause insomnia, restless sleep, and irregular sleep patterns. This prevents the body from getting adequate rest and can lead to reduced energy levels.

Discord in the family and strained relationships:

You must have noticed that in some homes, petty arguments and squabbles are a daily occurrence. Sometimes once a week, sometimes monthly, or even for several consecutive days. Why does this happen? Often, the reason is a lack of mutual love and respect. When family members don't show regard for each other, and if family members are involved in wrongful acts or illegal businesses, it affects the entire family atmosphere. Due to these wrong actions, there is a lack of peace and happiness in the home.

Yes, friends, money earned from wrongful deeds can also disrupt the peace of a home. Through actions that harm people instead of benefiting them, negative energy enters our lives. You might think these are mere imagination, but scientific facts also suggest that our thoughts and emotions have waves that deeply affect us and those around us.

Wrong actions not only impact our inner peace but can also shatter our personal and social relationships. When we act improperly towards someone, trust is broken, and it creates cracks in our relationships. People start distancing themselves from us because they sense our dishonesty or wrong behavior. This leads us to face loneliness and mental stress.

It often happens that people who get into the habit of wrongful actions try to hide them. This act of hiding continuously expends mental energy. Your mind is constantly under pressure, fearing that someone might discover your true nature. The mind has to work harder to conceal this continuous deception and pretense. This excessive mental exertion prevents us from fully utilizing our true potential.

And when this burden of pretense and concealment festers within us for a long time, gradually our mind and subconscious begin to tire. Their natural power diminishes. Because the energy that should have been used to maintain inner peace, that should have flowed into meditation and progress, and that was suitable for healing us from within—that very energy now starts to be wasted in concealing deceit and fear. The result is that the mind remains restless, contemplation is hindered, and the soul's innate healing power, which strengthens us from within, fades. Until we shed this burden, neither true peace nor the progress we inwardly yearn for in life can be found.

The human mind is naturally creative and powerful, but when we try to hide our wrongdoings and justify them, it cannot use its full power in the right direction. This is why we cannot accept our mistakes and naturally become irritable. Nothing seems good to us, and this mental disarray directly affects our relationships.

When we hide our wrong actions, we lose our inner peace and natural balance. This also makes our relationships strained and superficial. The more we remain trapped in wrongful deeds, the more our mental and emotional pressure increases, and the greater the distance in our relationships.

Scientific Research

Yes, there are also several scientific studies on this topic that explain this process. Research by **Axel Miles and Simon Titus** has found that when we try to hide our wrong actions, a mental stress called "cognitive dissonance" arises in our brain. This means that when our thoughts and actions do not align with each other, it leads to mental conflict. This conflict not only causes significant loss of our mental energy but also affects our emotional state and relationships.

Brain Science: Hans Berger's electroencephalography (EEG) experiments have proven that the electrical activities of the brain influence our mental stress. When we perform wrong actions and try to hide them, a large part of our mind remains busy in this conflict, which adversely affects our thoughts, emotions, and mental peace. This generates negativity in our aura and mental state.

Psychological Theory: In psychology, **Carl Jung** presented the theory of the "Shadow," according to which we unconsciously suppress our negative tendencies and actions. When we do not accept our mistakes or wrongdoings, it distorts our mental state and also creates tension in relationships. Jung's theory suggests that we should accept our weaknesses so that we can maintain mental and emotional balance.

Sociology: Erik Erikson, in his theory of psychosocial development, stated that if we behave wrongly towards others, it profoundly impacts our social relationships. This damages trust and self-esteem. Consequently, individuals find it difficult to accept themselves and others, which leads to cracks in relationships.

Financial losses:

Earned money through wrongful ways is not only unstable, but it also carries the influence of negative energy. When we deceive others, snatch away their rights, or earn money by causing them distress, their negative emotions—like anger, sorrow, or despair—become attached to our wealth. This negative energy can increase stress, unrest, and mental problems in our lives.

The Impact of Negative Energy

Spiritual organizations like Brahma Kumaris emphasize that food, clothes, and money all possess energy. Money acquired through wrongful means carries a greater negative energy influence. This is why they abstain from eating food at others' homes, believing that every item embodies the feelings and energy of the person who handled it.

This concept isn't limited to spirituality. Psychological research also suggests that when the source of wealth isn't ethical, individuals don't find satisfaction or happiness from it. A study by New York University found that money earned through unethical means increases stress, guilt, and mental instability.

Thoughts of Great Personalities

Gautam Buddha: "The ill effects of wealth and greed are that they make a person restless and discontent." Buddha emphasized earning wealth righteously. He believed that ill-gotten gains pollute our minds and deprive us of true happiness in life.

Osho: "Money has value, but only when it brings joy, peace, and love. Money earned wrongly poisons your life." According to Osho, when money is acquired through wrong means, it contaminates a person's aura, which increases negativity in life.

Swami Vivekananda: "It is essential for actions and wealth to be pure. Money gained through falsehood and injustice taints the soul." Vivekananda also explained that ill-gotten wealth leads only to sorrow and ignorance.

Scientific Research and Experiments

Emotion and Finance Research: This research shows that individuals who acquired wealth by harming or deceiving others exhibited more symptoms of depression and anxiety.

Masaru Emoto's Water Experiment: Japanese scientist Masaru Emoto demonstrated the effect of emotions on water. When water was exposed to positive energy (love and gratitude), its crystals were beautiful and organized. However, water exposed to negative energy (anger, hatred) showed scattered and distorted crystals. Similarly, objects like money and clothing also carry the influence of energy.

Nobel Laureate Daniel Kahneman: In his studies, he demonstrated that the source of wealth—whether ethical or unethical—impacts an individual's long-term happiness and mental health.

Spiritual and Scientific Perspectives

The impact of wealth earned through wrongful means isn't just on our external lives, but also on the **soul**. It pollutes our energy, which not only affects our thinking but also influences the people and relationships around us.

Earning wealth through right and ethical means not only brings financial stability but also fills our lives with positive energy and contentment. Remember, money is just a tool. Only wealth earned through righteous actions and honesty can bring true happiness and peace to our lives.

Money acquired through wrongful actions might offer immediate gains, but it brings long-term harm and negative energy. It affects not only our personal lives but also damages our relationships, mental health, and soul. Therefore, always pay attention to the means of earning wealth—because only money earned the right way brings true prosperity.

Mental burden

The impact of wrong actions is not limited to the external aspects of our lives; it profoundly affects our mind and brain. The guilt, dissatisfaction, and stress generated by wrongful deeds mentally exhaust us. This state not only disrupts our mental peace but also weakens the efficiency of our body and brain.

The Burden of Wrong Actions: Mental and Physical Effects

Pressure of Guilt and Anxiety

After committing wrongful acts, we have to make extra efforts to hide our mistakes and justify ourselves. This constant stress tires the brain. As Buddha said, "A person who carries the burden of lies can never find peace."

A 2018 study by Stanford University proved that guilt and lying cause our brain to continuously exert extra effort. In this process, pressure increases on the prefrontal cortex, which weakens our ability to make decisions and solve problems.

Memory and Mental Clarity

Due to wrong actions, our brain gets stuck in the process of "hiding mistakes." This makes us habitually forgetful, because our mind remains busy handling negativity instead of positive energy.

When you do wrong, your mind becomes restless, and a restless mind can never be creative.

Research has also shown that a long-term tendency to lie or hide wrong actions affects the hippocampus (the center of memory), which increases forgetfulness and mental weakness.

Impact on Physical and Mental Health

The mental burden of wrong actions pulls our brain's energy in a negative direction. A calm and happy mind performs wonders for the body, while a stressed mind pushes the body towards diseases.

Example:

A Harvard Medical School study found that the brain's response to stressful situations increases the level of cortisol (stress hormone), which weakens the immune system and can sometimes lead to high blood pressure and heart-related problems.

Wrong Actions and Obstruction in Right Decision-Making

The mental burden of wrong actions hinders our ability to think and make decisions. When the mind is burdened, it remains entangled even in small decisions.

Vivekananda said, "A calm mind is like a mirror; when it is disturbed, truth cannot be reflected in it."

From a scientific perspective, the executive function decreases in a restless mind, which weakens a person's decisions.

The Importance of Avoiding Wrong Actions

The mental burden created by wrong actions steals the joys of our life. When we do wrong, we not only harm ourselves, but the negative energy of others also affects us.

"As you sow, so shall you reap," this principle applies to every aspect of our lives. Organizations like Brahma Kumaris therefore avoid eating food at others' homes because they believe that every action and object carries energy. Money or food acquired through negative actions weakens us mentally and spiritually.

Lack of positivity

Wrong actions can lead to a deficiency of positivity in our lives. We become enveloped by negativity, which not only pollutes our thinking but also negatively impacts those around us. This creates a vicious cycle, trapping individuals and causing them to lose their inner peace, balance, and beauty. Gradually, our thoughts become frustrated, and discontent deepens in our hearts. In this state, we fail to attract positivity and peace into our lives.

Research and Experiments: The Impact of Mental Burden

Harvard University (2015):

This research found that individuals who repeatedly conceal their mistakes experience more mental fatigue compared to others. Brain scans clearly showed that the process of hiding expends a significant amount of brain energy, affecting both concentration and memory. Gradually, such a person becomes mentally exhausted, and even their inner peace starts feeling like a burden.

Duke University Experiment (2013):

This study revealed that in individuals who frequently lie and continuously engage in wrongful acts, the activity in the **prefrontal cortex**—the part of the brain responsible for ethics and discernment—decreases. This means that when someone repeatedly chooses the wrong path, their connection to their conscience gradually breaks down. They lose the sense of right and wrong, and even the power of repentance.

UCLA Neuroscience Research (2020):

Researchers found that in the absence of mental peace, the brain's **'default mode network'** fails to function properly. This network is essential for our creativity, self-reflection, and self-knowledge. When there is inner turmoil, no matter how the external world appears, everything feels incomplete and futile to the person. Such a mind cannot create; it can only run—from itself, from truth, and from life.

Gautam Buddha stated that the only way to attain peace in life is to acknowledge our sins and rectify them. Until a person learns to see and accept their inner mistakes, they cannot take a single step towards the soul's liberation.

Thoughts from Great Personalities on Right Actions

Buddha used to say, "As long as you run from your actions, your burden will not lighten."

Swami Vivekananda believed that truthfulness and purity are the foundations of mental health. He asserted that when a person repeatedly engages in lies and wrongful deeds, they are destroying both their body and mind. He clearly stated, "A soul that moves away from truth can never function with full strength."

Osho also explained that wrong actions not only alienate a person from themselves but also increase their distance from society and relationships. He said that a calm and innocent mind is the ground where the joy of life, love, and the experience of the divine are possible. Until the inner impurities are cleansed, external adornments are useless.

The Importance of Walking the Right Path

The mental burden created by wrong actions weakens the overall quality of our lives. It affects our memory, decision-making ability, and mental peace. To find lasting happiness and tranquility in life, embracing righteous actions is the simplest and most effective solution.

So friends, to avoid the mental burden of wrong actions, choose the path of right actions. This is the way that will lead you to true peace, contentment, and joy.

Chapter 05. Rebirth and Soul: Cycle of Karma

The principle of reincarnation is a philosophy of life's continuous journey. It's the belief that the **soul is immortal**, and the cycle of birth and death serves as a means for the soul's **progress and purification**. Leading religions, saints, thinkers, and scientists worldwide have presented their perspectives on this concept.

The soul has been regarded as an **eternal source of energy**. The Bhagavad Gita states:

"न जायते म्रियते वा कदाचित् , नायं भूत्वा भविता वा न भूयः।" (The soul is never born, nor does it ever die; it is primordial and immortal.)

According to modern science's law of **conservation of energy**, energy can neither be created nor destroyed. This aligns perfectly with the concept of the soul.

The Cycle of Soul and Karma

In Indian philosophy, the fundamental basis of **reincarnation** is **karma**. The Vedas and Upanishads state that the soul receives a new life as a result of its actions. This cycle continues until the soul attains its **perfection and liberation**.

Insights from Great Thinkers On Reincarnation

Mahatma Buddha: Buddha described reincarnation as part of the cycle of life and death, a consequence of karma. According to him, this cycle is broken only when an individual rises above their desires and wrong actions to attain Nirvana.

Osho: Osho viewed reincarnation as part of the soul's journey of development and experiences. He stated that the soul matures with new learnings in each birth, and its purpose is self-knowledge and the purification of the soul.

Swami Vivekananda: According to Vivekananda, the soul enters each new birth with its accumulated karma. Good actions elevate the soul, while bad actions bind it to the cycle of reincarnation.

Scientific Perspective and Evidence

Dr. Ian Stevenson: He studied over 3,000 cases where children recalled events from their previous lives. His research also found physical evidence corroborating these events.

Dr. Jim Tucker: While researching children's past-life memories, he found that these were not mere imagination but profound experiences.

Dr. Brian Weiss: In his book Many Lives, Many Masters, he explained that past-life memories influence present-day life and can even serve as a medium for therapy.

Reincarnation Experiences and Incidents

The Case of Shanti Devi (India)

This case is one of the most widely discussed examples of reincarnation. A girl named Shanti Devi recalled details of her previous life and spoke about her former family. After investigating the veracity of her statements, it was proven that the details she provided were correct. Many prominent leaders also showed interest in this case, and it gained international attention.

James Leininger (USA)

A young boy named James recalled experiences as a World War II pilot in his previous life. He provided details about his plane crash and mentioned several facts about his past life, which were later found to be true. This incident drew many people's attention to the concept of reincarnation.

Cases of Peculiar Dreams and Recognizing Places

Many people describe dreams or places about which they have no information in their current life. When they visit these places, they feel fragments of past-life memories.

Purpose of Reincarnation

Reincarnation is not merely a part of the soul's journey; it is the path of the soul's evolution and purification. It explains that only by performing right actions can the soul reach higher states.

Reincarnation is the soul's continuous journey, offering us an opportunity to understand our actions and their effects. It presents life as a responsibility, where right actions become the path to the soul's progress and liberation.

The soul is immortal, karma is its companion, and the cycle of birth and death is its path. This journey is completed only when the soul comes to know itself.

Akashic Records

The Akashic Records can be understood as an invisible book of life and the cosmos, containing a comprehensive record of every thought, action, experience, and emotion of every soul across all its births. This is a type of cosmic data that helps in understanding the soul's journey and provides guidance for spiritual development.

In ancient Indian texts, the word 'Akasha' is mentioned, meaning "etheric element" or "subtlest field." According to modern definitions, Akashic Records are considered an energy field that encompasses every soul's karma, experiences, and developmental journey. They can also be viewed as a vast database of actions.

Principles of Akashic Records

Akashic Records indicate that our every action, every thought, and every emotion is recorded in the universe as a form of energy. This energy is not destroyed; rather, it is preserved in this invisible realm of the cosmos.

Individual Account for Every Soul: Every individual has their own "spiritual account." It records everything they have thought, felt, and done in every birth.

Guidance for the Future: Based on these records, our karma determines the direction of our life in subsequent births.

Principle of Cause and Effect: Akashic Records determine the next stages of life based on the fruits of karma.

Science and Akashic Records

Although Akashic Records are a spiritual concept, many scientific and spiritual researchers have attempted to understand and validate them.

Edgar Cayce: Known as the "Sleeping Prophet," Edgar Cayce claimed to access the Akashic Records. He would enter a trance state and provide information about people's past lives and their karma. Many researchers believe that a type of energy exists in the universe that records every event and every action. This energy might exist in the cosmos in the form of our DNA or quantum energy.

Akashic Records and Reincarnation

Akashic Records have a deep connection with reincarnation. It is believed that when a soul takes on a new life, it carries its past actions and experiences from the Akashic Records.

If a soul performed good deeds in a past life, it receives positive energy and circumstances in its next life. If it performed negative actions, it faces difficulties to balance them out.

Modern Experiments and Experiences

Dolores Cannon: Dolores Cannon was a renowned author and researcher in the field of reincarnation. She uncovered stories of hundreds of people's past lives using Akashic Records.

Michael Newton: Michael Newton wrote the book "Journey of Souls," in which he explained in detail the journey of souls and the role of Akashic Records.

Raymond Moody: Raymond Moody included descriptions of near-death experiences (NDEs) and the soul's journey in his book "Life After Life."

Importance of Akashic Records

Helps in Understanding Life: This helps us understand the impact of our actions and accept their consequences.

Spiritual Development: Knowledge of Akashic Records inspires us to improve our actions and purify the soul.

Direction and Purpose: This helps us understand that our life is not limited to material pleasures but is a means for the soul's progress and development.

Conclusion

Akashic Records teach us that our actions not only affect our present life but also play a significant role in the soul's endless journey. This knowledge inspires us to understand that every action has importance, and every thought, every emotion becomes a part of the cosmic energy. When we understand this, we gain the power to guide our lives in the right direction.

Chapter 06. Karma Yoga and Types of Karma

Every morning when the sun rises, it selflessly gives light to the entire world. It doesn't discriminate who uses its light and who doesn't. Similarly, Karma Yoga teaches us that our actions should be just like that—**selfless, without expectation of reward**.

Karma Yoga: A Way of Life

Krishna told Arjuna, "You have the right to perform your prescribed duty, but you are not entitled to the fruits of action." This verse teaches us that success or failure in life doesn't matter as much as performing our duties with complete honesty and dedication.

Imagine a farmer sowing seeds in their field. They don't work thinking about whether it will rain or not. They simply do their duty. Karma Yoga is the essence of this feeling—we should perform our work in the best possible way, but **without worrying about its outcome**.

Types of Karma: A Detailed Analysis

1. Sanchita Karma (Accumulated Karma):

Sanchita Karma refers to the actions accumulated by the soul over many lifetimes, clinging to it like a subtle treasury. This treasury is filled with both good and bad deeds. Whether we performed a virtuous act or a sin in any birth, its record remains securely stored in this treasury. The fruit of these actions isn't received immediately, but when the time comes, we must experience them—be it good or bad, in various forms. This is the unchangeable law of divine justice: "**The fruit of every action is certain, no matter how old it may be.**"

2. Prarabdha Karma (Destined Karma):

Prarabdha Karma is that specific portion of our accumulated karma that the soul carries into a new birth to experience in this life. These are the actions that determine the circumstances of our current life: our birthplace, family, physical condition, and initial joys and sorrows.

If the accumulated Sanchita Karma contains more virtue, then Prarabdha might be pleasant. However, if the soul takes birth with a specific learning objective, it may also choose difficulties for itself. For example, if a person is born blind, it may not solely be the result of past sin—it could also be that their soul resolved to learn some deep spiritual lesson through the experience of blindness in this life.

3. Kriyamana Karma (Present Karma):

Kriyamana Karma refers to the new actions we perform daily in this life—through thoughts, speech, and deeds. These are the most powerful tools in our hands because our future is created from them. The fruits of some Kriyamana Karma are experienced in this very life, while others become part of future Sanchita or Prarabdha. This is why we should act with awareness every moment, as these present actions determine the direction of our next birth and spiritual evolution. If we perform righteous deeds, not only will our life improve, but our soul will also ascend.

Interconnectedness of Karma Types

- Our Sanchita Karma determines our Prarabdha.
- Our Prarabdha influences our current life.
- Our Kriyamana Karma sows seeds for our future and affects our Sanchita Karma.

Importance of Karma Principle:

The principle of karma tells us that our actions have a profound impact on our lives. It motivates us to perform good deeds. It also teaches us that we can better our future through our actions.The principle of karma is a deep and complex subject. It's not easy to understand it completely. But, it gives us a new perspective on our lives. It teaches us to be responsible for our actions and inspires us to live a better life.

Difference Between Karma and Destiny:

Karma and destiny are often seen as intertwined, but there's a significant difference between the two. **Karma** is the result of our own efforts, while **destiny** is considered predetermined. The principle of karma teaches us that we can change our destiny through our actions.

Impact of Karma Principle on Modern Life:

Even in the modern age, the importance of the karma principle has not diminished. This principle helps us understand and face life's ups and downs. It teaches us:

- **Responsibility:** We are responsible for our own lives.
- **Good Deeds:** Performing good deeds betters our future.
- **Patience:** The fruits of actions aren't immediate; we need to be patient.
- **Negative Thoughts:** Negative thoughts influence our actions.
- **Service to Others:** Serving others brings us mental peace.

How to Improve Karma:

To improve our karma, we can take the following steps:

- **Positive Thinking:** Always maintain positive thoughts.
- **Helping Others:** Helping others brings us happiness.
- **Speaking Truth:** Speaking the truth is always good.
- **Non-violence:** We should avoid violence.
- **Gaining Knowledge:** Acquiring knowledge helps us make better decisions.
- **Meditation and Yoga:** Practicing meditation and yoga calms the mind, enabling us to perform good deeds.

The principle of karma helps us become better individuals and build a better society. It teaches us that our actions shape our future. Therefore, we should always strive to perform good deeds. When we understand that every action has a consequence, we become more aware of what we are doing.

Karma Yoga and Balance

The essence of Karma Yoga is the **balance of action and contemplation**. It's not just about performing your work with full dedication, but also understanding *why* you are doing it. If we work only to earn money, we quickly get tired. But if our purpose is the welfare of others, the same work energizes us.

A Simple Story

Manish and Raju, two office colleagues, were walking home late one evening, the last ones to leave the office. Suddenly, Manish remembered he had forgotten to switch off the electricity in the office. "Raju, I have to go back," he said, "I forgot to turn off the power. It'll prevent wasting electricity and keep our office light bill from increasing."

Raju looked at him, puzzled. "Why are you doing this, Manish? We're just small office workers, not the owners. It's not our loss, so why bother?"

Manish shook his head. "No, I have to do this. It's not right if I don't."

Raju persisted, "But there's no one watching you, and no one's going to give you a reward for this good work."

Manish smiled gently. "I'm not doing this for any reward, and I don't care if anyone is watching or not. I am watching, and my soul is also watching. I'm doing this for my own inner peace." With that, Manish turned back and went to switch off the power in the office.

Karma Yoga in Modern Life

In today's busy life, we often get so engrossed in worrying about the outcome that we forget to enjoy the work itself.

If you are a teacher, focus on teaching your students, not on their grades. If you are a parent, give your child love and guidance, don't just focus on their achievements.

The True Meaning of Karma Yoga

Karma Yoga doesn't just mean performing good deeds; it means performing every action with **honesty, selflessness, and mindfulness**. Just as a gardener tends to their plants, we should tend to our actions. In every situation of life, our every small or big action, every thought, and every word is karma. These actions shape our future. Therefore, it's crucial for us to understand that karma is not limited to physical activity; it remains continuously active through our thoughts, words, and actions.

Mostly we are doing Three Types of Karma

1. Thinking and Feeling (Karma of the Mind):

Our **thoughts and emotions** are the very first form of karma. What we think influences our energy and the direction of our lives. If we harbor hatred or jealousy towards someone in our minds, this negative energy affects our lives. Conversely, positive thinking and compassion lead us toward inner peace and happiness.

When you have a desire to help someone, that thought brings peace to your mind. However, if you hold negative feelings for someone, it makes you restless internally. Therefore, keeping your thoughts pure is also an important action.

2. Speaking (Karma of Speech):

Our **words are like arrows**—once released, they can't be taken back. The impact of our speech profoundly affects those around us and the world. Discouraging words can cast a negative shadow on someone's life, while inspiring and positive words can uplift and shape a life for the better.

If a child is repeatedly told, "You can't achieve anything in life," it plants a seed of negativity in their mind. That child might then begin to doubt their own capabilities. In contrast, if you say, "You have the potential to achieve something great," they can find the courage to move forward in life.

Remember, **speech is also karma**. Always think before you speak about what impact your words might have on someone's life.

3. Physical Actions (Physical Form of Karma):

Our thoughts and words ultimately transform into **physical actions**. Working hard, helping someone, or moving towards your goal are positive actions. Conversely, harming someone, engaging in violence, or deliberately doing wrong are negative actions.

A farmer working hard in their field is performing a physical action. Their hard work not only benefits their own life but also affects others by providing food.

On the other hand, if someone engages in violence or deliberately harms another, they create a negative impact on both their own life and the lives of others.

The Interconnection of Karma

Thought, speech, and action—these three types of karma are deeply interconnected.

1. As you think, so you speak.

2. As you speak, so you act.

3. Ultimately, your actions shape your future.

Therefore, if you want to make your karma pure and positive, first purify your thoughts. Maintain peace and compassion in your mind. Make your speech inspiring and positive. Perform your actions selflessly.

The Essence of Karma Yoga

Karma Yoga teaches us that every action in life, whether it's a **thought, a word, or a deed**, should be done mindfully and responsibly.

Consider the impact your thoughts and words will have on others. Remember that your actions matter not just for you, but for the world as well.

Every action, whether small or large, creates a ripple in the world. Strive to make this ripple positive and peaceful.

Chapter 07. Good & Bad Karma: Comparison

Identifying and comparing good and bad actions is one of life's profound questions. Understanding what truly constitutes a "good" or "bad" action isn't always easy. Our thoughts and circumstances can often lead to confusion. To arrive at the correct definition of good and bad karma, we need to evaluate every situation and its consequences not just superficially, but deeply.

Good actions are those that bring positive change to others' lives, make them better, and provide long-term benefit. Conversely, bad actions are those that have a negative impact on others' lives, cause suffering, or prove harmful to society and oneself. However, this definition doesn't apply to every situation, as the determination of right and wrong isn't solely based on intentions, but also on outcomes.

For example, when we give money to a beggar, at first glance, it appears to be a good deed. We think we've helped someone in need. But if we think deeper and understand the beggar's background, things might change. If that beggar is responsible for their current situation because they chose to shirk their responsibilities, caused distress to their family, and ruined their life due to habits like alcohol, gambling, and laziness, then giving them money might actually worsen their situation.

Suppose if the beggar receives a lot of money today, they might revert to their old bad habits. They might bother others and not benefit themselves or society. In such a scenario, giving them money, which we usually consider a good deed, could actually become a bad action. This is because your help might empower a wrong person to potentially harm others again.

Therefore, when comparing good and bad actions, one

should focus not just on emotions, but on facts and consequences. Helping those in need is good, but it's also crucial to ensure that our help is utilized appropriately. Any action can only be considered good if its outcome is positive and benefits society.

Discerning Karma and Its Truth

When we categorize an action as good or bad, it's not solely dependent on its outward appearance. The true evaluation of an action hinges on its underlying **motive, feeling, and consequences**. Genuine actions are those that purify the soul and are beneficial to society.

Consider, for example, a person who goes to the temple every day. People see them as religious, honest, and kind. But if they do this merely to cultivate an image, hoping others will praise them and consider them superior, then this action might not be truly good. This action isn't a means of spiritual growth; it's a **display of ego**.

Pretense not only corrupts the soul but also creates illusion for others. Such an individual performs actions to appear good in the eyes of others, but their soul remains hollow within. This action might look good externally, but its roots lie in deceit and falsehood.

Identifying True Karma

True actions originate from within, expecting neither praise nor any personal gain.

A person who secretly helps someone, simply because they feel it's their duty, performs true actions. If you try to make yourself look great through your actions, that's not good karma; it's beyond mere pretense. Actions that genuinely improve society and individual life are the ones that elevate the soul.

Every action impacts society and the soul. Actions driven by pretense not only set a wrong example in society but also lead the soul towards decline. On the other hand, even the smallest actions performed with honesty and sincerity can have a profound impact.

For instance, giving food to a poor person is a good deed. But if this food is given only so people will consider you kind, then this act of giving food becomes a **selfish action**. However, if you do it without any desire for publicity or praise, this very action elevates your soul.

Evaluating Your Actions

When performing an action, it's crucial to examine your intentions. Ask yourself:

- Am I doing this simply for my image?
- Will this action truly benefit someone?
- Will this action bring satisfaction to my soul?

The Importance of Truthfulness in Life

Truthfulness and sincerity are the foundation of good karma. If you rise above the facade of pretense and act with honesty, your soul will reach a higher level. Good actions purify the soul and leave a positive impact on society.

Therefore, be mindful at every step. Understand the subtle difference between pretense and truth. Evaluate your actions and ensure they are uplifting for your soul.

When identifying karma, we must keep our understanding alert. Sometimes, an action that is good in one situation can become bad in another. Thus, a true understanding of good and bad karma is only possible after deep thought and properly assessing every situation.

For instance, if a woman leaves her husband and home to elope with someone else, society generally deems it a bad action. It's a violation of family, relationships, and social values. However, when we consider her circumstances—if her husband is an alcoholic, abuses her, her mother-in-law harasses her, and she has never received love, respect, or a happy life—it becomes clear that she is merely taking a step for her own existence and happiness.

Determining Bad Karma Based on Context

No action can be judged as good or bad solely by its immediate result or impact. We must also consider the **intention and reasons** behind that action.

- **If she fled to escape abuse and suffering:** This is an act of self-preservation and protection of her right to live. In such a case, it's not a bad action, but an attempt at self-defense.
- **If she fled for a selfish purpose:** If she has dont have any problem in femily but she took this step merely for more wealth, luxury, or to fulfill her desires, then it could be considered wrong.

True Understanding of Good and Bad

Everyone in the world has the right to be happy. Forcibly keeping someone in a situation where they are tormented and their dignity is hurt is, in itself, a sin.

Everyone has the right to be happy, and if they have to take drastic measures to free themselves from their bonds, it cannot be called a bad action. We should always assess karma based on its intention and the circumstances, not just on the external outcome.

This is why understanding the knowledge of karma deeply is crucial.

Understanding the true knowledge and depth of karma is essential for every individual. We often judge karma as good or bad merely by its superficial layer. But in reality, the roots of karma lie in intention, circumstances, and its long-term effects.

Three Bases for Deeply Understanding Karma:

1. Intention:

The root of every action lies in its intention. If the intention is pure, for the well-being of others, then the action will be considered good. If the intention involves selfishness, hatred, or the desire to harm someone, then the action becomes bad. Example: Speaking the truth to help someone is good karma. But if the same truth is spoken to intentionally humiliate someone, it can become bad karma.

2. Circumstance (Context):

Without understanding the circumstances, it's impossible to properly assess an action. The criteria for right and wrong can change with each situation. Example: If a poor person steals because they have nothing to eat, the theft might be morally wrong, but based on the circumstances, it wouldn't be fair to call them a criminal.

3. Consequence (Long-term Impact):

The result of an action should be judged not only by its immediate effect but also by its long-term impact. Example: If someone's life is saved by telling a lie, that lie would be considered a good action.

Why is True Knowledge of Karma Essential?

The true knowledge of karma empowers us to make right decisions in life. We cannot evaluate karma by being bound by societal conventions and limitations. The distinction between right and wrong can only be understood through discernment, sensitivity, and a deep study of karma.

Friends, this knowledge of karma should not be limited to just listening, reading, or understanding. Apply it in your life.

Every day, every moment, introspect your actions. Think:

- Is my action right?
- Is it beneficial for me and for others?
- Is it appropriate according to my intention, circumstances, and potential outcomes?

Remember, the true knowledge of karma can free you from every dilemma in life.

Chapter 08. The Path of the Seer

The path of the Seer is an experience beyond karma. Beyond the confines of good and bad deeds, the Seer's path offers us the opportunity to witness the true nature of life. Often, we become so entangled in the web of our actions that we lose sight of life's entire meaning. Bad karma pulls our soul into darkness and degradation. It disturbs us from within, filling our minds with anxiety, guilt, and turmoil. These actions push us into a deep vortex of ignorance and negativity, disrupting our inner peace and alienating us from our true selves.

Conversely, good karma elevates our soul. It inspires us towards peace, contentment, and spiritual growth. These actions fill us with compassion and love, spreading positive energy around us. However, between these two extremes lies a path that allows us neither to get lost in goodness nor entangled in negativity. This is the **path of becoming a Seer**, where we experience life merely as a witness, free from the consequences of our actions.

What Does It Mean to Be a Seer?

To become a Seer means to perceive oneself as a witness, beyond all actions and their results. It's understanding that we are merely characters in this world, and everything that unfolds is like a play. This is a deep spiritual truth that liberates us from ego and attachment. The first step to becoming a Seer is to detach yourself from the emotional impact of your actions. It's knowing that every experience is a fleeting moment, meant only to be observed, not lived. Often, we identify so strongly with our actions that we can't help but be affected by their outcomes. But as a Seer, you observe your actions like the flow of a river – they keep moving, and you stand on the bank, watching them.

When you become a Seer, you don't weigh actions on the scales of right or wrong. You simply observe them in their natural form. This neutrality frees you from the bonds of karma and grants you an inner freedom untouched by any circumstance. It's a deep understanding that you are merely an observer, and the drama of life unfolds before you.

The Importance of Neutrality and Inner Peace

The greatest benefit of becoming a Seer is the experience of neutrality. Neutrality doesn't mean you are irresponsible or inactive. It means you are free from the ego of action and the fear of consequences. You act in your pure form, without any desire for gain, praise, or punishment. Action then becomes your nature, not a burden. This is the state where action itself becomes joy.

When you are a Seer, you detach yourself from the effects of your actions. Good karma often gives rise to ego – the feeling of "I did this good deed." Bad karma causes guilt and regret – "I wish I hadn't done that." But when you are a Seer, you rise above both. You see karma merely as an action, without any emotional attachment. This neutrality provides you with inner peace and stability, as you are free from the worry of outcomes. It's a state where you accept every event in life, whether pleasant or unpleasant, and simply view them as experiences.

View life merely as a witness. Whatever is happening, see it from the outside, not from within. Just like you're enjoying a movie. You connect with the characters, but you know it's just a story. To become a Seer means to observe life without any interference, without trying to control it. When you become merely a witness, action itself transforms into spiritual practice. Then, there's no burden of good karma, nor the remorse of bad karma. This is a state of liberation where you remain unattached even while performing actions.

Practicing the Path of the Seer: Awaken Your Consciousness

The path of becoming a Seer is not an overnight attainment, but rather a continuous practice. Here are some simple and effective exercises to awaken your consciousness:

- **Sit quietly for some time each day.** Choose a comfortable place where no one will disturb you. This could be in the morning, or before going to sleep.
- **Observe your thoughts, feelings, and actions without judgment.** When a thought arises, don't label it as good or bad. Just observe it, like you watch clouds drifting in the sky. Observe your emotions in the same way – anger, joy, sorrow – feel them, but don't get lost in them.
- **Observe actions passively.** When you do something, don't see yourself as the doer of that action, but rather observe it happening. For example, if you are washing dishes, just focus on the sound of the water, the feel of the dishes, and the smell of the soap, without the thought of "I am washing dishes."
- **Understand that your actions are not "yours."** They are merely a part of the flow of life. You are a medium through which actions occur. This is a deep belief that frees you from ego.
- **Take deep breaths and meditate.** Meditation connects you to the truth that "you" are merely the witness. Focus on

your breath – the incoming and outgoing breath. When your mind wanders, gently bring it back to your breath. This practice will help you stay in the present moment and connect with your inner Seer.

- **Be mindful:** Strive to be mindful in all your daily activities. When you eat, savor every bite. When you walk, feel your feet on the ground. This mindfulness will help you detach from your experiences and observe them purely as a witness.

Conclusion: The Ultimate Truth of Life

The path of the Seer is the simplest and most effective means to deeply understand life and find its true meaning. It not only purifies our soul but also liberates us from the cycle of karma. This is a liberation that takes us beyond the bondage of birth and death. When you become a Seer, you view life as a game, and you remain a spectator even while being a player in that game.

Remember, becoming a Seer means knowing yourself. It is the path of self-realization. And when you recognize your true reality, all questions about life automatically cease. You understand that you are much more than your body, mind, or emotions – you are an eternal, infinite consciousness that merely witnesses every experience. This is the state where you experience complete joy and peace, as you connect with your true self. The path of the Seer is not just a spiritual concept, but a practical way of living that allows you to experience peace and freedom in every moment.

Chapter 09. Practicing Good Deeds Daily

People often say that doing good deeds is difficult. And it's true, our minds and habits constantly pull us back to old patterns. But there's a simple and effective solution that can make this difficulty easy: **meditation**.

Make meditation a part of your life.

Meditation is a tool that gradually calms the negative thoughts and wrong desires hidden within us. To understand this, imagine dirty water in a pot settling over time, with the debris sinking to the bottom, leaving clear water on top. The same process happens in our minds through meditation. The "debris" within us—anger, jealousy, greed, and negativity—slowly settles, and the mind's inherent purity begins to manifest in our thoughts and actions.

Meditation not only calms the mind but also provides an experience of connecting with the depths of the soul. It fills our heart and mind with positivity. When we meditate regularly, the desire for wrong actions naturally diminishes. Furthermore, if we ever make a mistake unknowingly, meditation makes us so aware that we can recognize that mistake and try to correct it.

Meditation connects us to the divine and makes us realize that we are a small but significant part of this universe. This experience helps us understand the difference between right and wrong. Meditation frees us from ego and fear, allowing us to make better decisions and improve our lives.

The Connection Between Meditation and Karma

Meditation not only purifies our mind but also reflects in our actions.

When the mind is calm and clear, decisions are also sound. Meditation teaches us to understand and act thoughtfully in any situation, rather than just reacting.

Meditation isn't just an exercise; it's a way of life. It teaches us that every moment is important and that it's possible to do the right thing in every moment. By connecting with meditation, we can improve our daily actions and purify our soul.

Remember, good deeds aren't just for external show; they're for inner contentment and peace of soul. And meditation is the simplest and most powerful tool to achieve this peace and balance.

Embrace meditation. Don't consider it a difficult or rigid process; it's an incredibly easy and simple way to make your life even better. As you go deeper into meditation, your actions naturally begin to improve. The inner peace and awareness gained from meditation keep you on the right path. And this is what makes your life meaningful and joyful.

If you find it hard to improve your actions, understand that no change happens in a day. It's a journey, and every journey begins with a small step. Meditation is your greatest companion in this.

Through meditation, negative thoughts hidden deep within the mind begin to subside, and a flow of positivity begins. But if you've been performing wrong actions for a long time and now wish to change, you'll need **patience and firm determination**. Assume that you might fail repeatedly in the beginning. However, despite every failure, maintain the firm belief within you that you will continue to strive towards righteous actions.

Ways to Change Bad Habits

- **Practice Meditation:** Start meditation for a short time, perhaps 5-10 minutes initially, and gradually increase the duration every 10-20 days. Slowly extend it to half an hour or an hour. Meditation will awaken an inner strength that will help you break free from bad habits and actions.
- **Control Your Speech:** Be mindful of your words. Speak thoughtfully. Understand what impact your words will have on others and how they will affect the future. Always keep your language full of **love, kindness, and truth**.
- **Visualize the Future:** Before acting, visualize the outcome of your words and deeds in your mind. Think about the impact of whatever you do. This practice will help you avoid wrong actions and give you the ability to make correct decisions.
- **Control Your Thoughts:** Just as controlling speech is essential, controlling your thoughts is also necessary. Always think positively. Aim to do good for others. Free your mind from negative thoughts like deceit, fraud, or conspiracy. Even if someone deceives you, don't dwell on it. Don't let their mistake overpower you.

The Miraculous Effect of Karma

Remember, whatever karma you perform will come back to you—and likely amplified. If you've done good deeds, they will bring happiness, peace, and prosperity into your life. And if you've done wrong, their consequences can be equally intense and difficult.

As you begin to control your thoughts, words, and actions,

you'll see your life transform. Miracles will start manifesting around you. Your relationships will improve, and the feeling of joy and contentment in life will grow.

This journey of right actions might be challenging, but it will not only make your life better but also purify your soul. This journey will connect you to the true purpose of life.

Chapter 10. Development of Society & Nation

The development of a society and nation isn't measured solely by grand structures, buildings, or economic progress. True development is what brings about change within every individual, fostering purity and positivity in their thoughts and actions. Until an ordinary citizen embraces good deeds in their life, society will only see external changes, not internal prosperity. This chapter illuminates how right actions can form the foundation of development, from individual lives to a national scale.

Beyond Economic Progress

Economic advancement is a crucial aspect of development, but it alone isn't sufficient. True development occurs when the benefits of this economic prosperity reach all sections of society. If an individual brings change to society through their actions—like helping the poor, promoting education, or protecting the environment—this is far more valuable than mere economic progress. A nation's true progress is based on the moral values and actions of its citizens.

Social Harmony and Right Actions

Right actions foster a sense of trust and love in society. When every individual understands their responsibility towards their neighbors, their community, and their nation, a positive energy flows through society. This energy not only unites the community but also reduces problems like crime, corruption, and inequality.

The Importance of Education and Ethics

Education is the foundation of society. But education

shouldn't be limited to earning degrees. It's essential to include moral and social responsibilities. If children are taught about good deeds and their impact from a young age, they will not only become better citizens but also bring about positive change in society. Prioritizing moral education in schools and universities is a vital part of true development.

Health and Sanitation

Only a healthy society can progress. Maintaining cleanliness around us and raising awareness about it is a small but effective way of performing right actions. When people take care of their health and inspire others to do the same, it impacts the entire society. This isn't just an individual responsibility but a collective effort.

Leadership and Inspiration

Individuals who perform right actions become a source of inspiration in society. Their deeds motivate others, and this inspiration can bring about change across the entire community. A good leader is one who not only performs right actions themselves but also guides others in the right direction through their conduct. Think of leaders like Dr. APJ Abdul Kalam, whose entire life was a testament to selfless action and dedication to national progress. His focus wasn't just on scientific achievements, but on inspiring every young mind to contribute to India's bright future through ethical conduct.

Your Role in the Development of Society and Nation

Every individual has an opportunity to contribute to the development of society and the nation. This contribution can be made not only through grand gestures but also through small actions. For example, helping someone in need, educating children, or protecting the environment. These small efforts have a long-lasting impact and bring about significant change.

Beyond Individual Actions: Collective Transformation

To make the nation even stronger and more prosperous, we need to embrace some bigger and more profound changes. When individuals are truly good and righteous, they will choose an honest and capable leader for the nation with full integrity. If corruption does exist, a **conscious citizenry** in a **conscious nation** will easily be able to curb such practices. Furthermore, this foundation of good karma will foster brotherhood and understanding among people of different faiths.

Conclusion

The development of society and the nation is a collective effort. It is every individual's responsibility to bring positivity into society through their actions. When every citizen understands their responsibility and works in the right direction, the nation will experience not only external progress but also internal prosperity. This is true development, where every individual is happy, society is peaceful, and the nation becomes self-reliant.

Chapter 11. Teaching good Karma in Education

Karma is the fundamental essence of life. It's the outcome of our actions, thoughts, and conduct. Every person, whether a child or an adult, shapes their future through their karma. It's crucial to understand and feel that good and bad actions profoundly impact our lives. In today's modern age, where people are mostly motivated by material progress, imparting the right education about karma to children is essential. In this context, the importance of schools increases because that's where children's mental and moral development takes place. If we can teach our children about the significance of karma from childhood, we can show them a path to living a strong and positive life.

The Importance of Karma Education

Nowadays, the objective of educational institutions shouldn't just be to make children academically competent, but also to focus on their moral and social development. If a child understands **right actions**, they will not only be successful in life but will also comprehend their responsibility towards society. Karma education teaches children that whatever is happening in life is a result of their past actions. Good karma brings peace, balance, and self-confidence into life, while bad karma leads us to inner turmoil and regret.

Objectives of Karma Education:

To help children understand the difference between good and bad actions. To develop children's ability to make right decisions. To make children ethical and compassionate. To make them realize their responsibilities towards society and family. To teach children that every action has a consequence, and we should take steps thoughtfully, considering the results of our actions.

Integrating Karma Education in Schools

Schools shouldn't just teach children subjects like mathematics, science, and other academic topics; they should also impart moral education and karma education. This education guides their lives in a better direction and makes them good citizens in society. If we want to bring about change in our society, it's necessary to make children aware of the impact and importance of their actions from childhood itself.

How Can Karma Education Be Integrated?

Subjects related to ethics and karma can be added to the curriculum. The impact of karma can be explained through dialogues and discussions among children. Karma education can be instilled in children's minds through stories and examples. Children can be encouraged to think about and understand good and bad actions by forming small groups in the classroom.

Karma Education and Child Personality Development

When children are taught about good deeds, their personality also develops in a positive direction. They not only understand their duties towards their family but also strive to direct their actions correctly in society. Karma education strengthens both their self-confidence and morality. Through this education, children are taught that not just academic success, but right conduct and actions are also important in life.

Benefits of Karma Education

- **Positive Mindset:** When children are told about the importance of good actions, they bring positive changes to their thinking. They desire to do good not only for themselves but also for others.

- **Contribution to Society:** Karma education helps children understand that they are part of society and their actions affect it. Through good deeds, they can bring positive change in society.
- **Self-Control:** Karma education increases self-control and self-confidence in children. They think about the consequences before undertaking any task.
- **Moral Responsibility:** Children develop a sense of responsibility. They understand that every action has an impact and they try to evaluate their actions correctly.

Long-Term Impact of Karma Education

When children receive proper karma education, its impact lasts throughout their lives. As they grow up, they become individuals who contribute to society. This education teaches them that success in life is achieved not only through hard work but also through **honesty, kindness, and responsibility**.

Contribution of Teachers

For karma education to be effective in schools, the **contribution of teachers is very important**. Teachers not only impart academic knowledge to children but also guide their lives. When teachers set an example of good deeds through their conduct, children understand that right actions are done not just through words, but also through deeds. Teachers are role models for children, and children learn from their behavior how to perform true actions in life.

Integrating karma education in schools is not only essential for the moral and mental development of children but also plays a significant role in the development of society and the nation. When children understand the impact of karma and internalize it in their lives, they become **empowered, responsible, and wise citizens**. Karma education comprehensively develops children's personalities, guiding their lives in a positive direction. This is the foundation that leads them towards success, peace, and contentment in life.

Chapter 12. The Path to Living a beautiful life

If we learn the art of living with **love and peace**, most of life's problems begin to solve themselves. Life will feel both beautiful and easy.

Simply earning money, building a beautiful house, or getting a high-paying job isn't the true source of happiness and peace. We've seen how many lives, despite having all these things, remain filled with difficulties and stress. Why? Because they don't know the path to living with peace and love.

Here, I'm trying to explain this to you simply. you must have seen many homes where there's constant conflict—small arguments, and a severe lack of mutual affection. In such an environment, no matter how many material comforts there are, contentment and joy cannot truly enter life.

To live a good and truthful life, we must first take steps towards understanding ourselves. We must accept the truth that we are not here merely for material goals, but that the true purpose of our life is a spiritual journey. We are reborn repeatedly so that our soul can be further refined, so that we can reach a higher level from the soul's perspective. The goal of our soul is to better itself and attain higher consciousness.

Therefore, make a place for **meditation** in your life. Through meditation, you can raise your level of consciousness. And when your consciousness rises, all other things—happiness, peace, love, solutions—will naturally and effortlessly come into your life.

If you have families in your home or neighborhood where there's never peace, where there's a lack of mutual affection and often an atmosphere of conflict—you can learn an important lesson from them.

Those people are unknowingly your teachers, showing you what not to do in life. By observing their experiences, you can decide that you will not let such situations arise in your own life. If you constantly harbor negative feelings, anger, hatred, or malice towards anyone in your mind, you are actually doing the greatest injustice to yourself.

So keep your mind clear and pure towards everyone. Forgive everyone from the heart. Have feelings of love for everyone. Because this is the true nature of our soul—**pure love and deep peace**.

This is, in essence, the path to living with love and peace. Peace and love are two such wonderful elements of life that not only balance our existence but also create a sense of happiness and contentment within us and in the external world. The importance of these two in life increases even more when we understand the cycle of karma and realize that the greatest purpose of life is to establish a deep connection with ourselves and others through peace and love. Peace and love not only make our individual lives beautiful but also make an invaluable contribution to the well-being of society and the nation.

Practice Meditation

Meditation is the most effective way to walk the path of peace and love. Through meditation, we can calm our minds and feel love and peace deep within. It provides us with mental clarity and makes our outlook on life positive.

Increase Empathy and Understanding Towards Others

When we try to understand others' perspectives and show

empathy in their circumstances, we expand love and peace. This not only strengthens our relationships but also fosters a sense of unity and harmony in society.

Self-Acceptance

We must also see ourselves with love and peace. **Self-cultivation and self-respect** are an integral part of practicing peace and love. When we truly accept ourselves and recognize the good within us, peace and love automatically enter our lives.

Let Go of Anger and Hatred

Every person has good and bad experiences in life. When we are angry with someone or hate them, we expend our energy in a negative direction. Therefore, we need to remove anger and hatred from our minds and replace them with peace and love.

Impact of Peace and Love on Society

When we adopt peace and love in our lives, it also impacts society. When we have good relationships with others, help them, and behave with love, an atmosphere of peace is created in society. This lays the foundation for a strong society, where people help each other, understand each other, and work with a sense of unity.

Chapter 13. Karmic Energy at Your Workplace

Every action we take emits its own energy waves, which not only affect our lives but are also connected to the place, society, and world where that action is performed. The accumulation and flow of this energy determine the outcomes of our karma. When we act, that energy gathers at that location, and this energy can be either positive or negative. This very karmic energy influences our soul, body, and mental state, and also impacts the collective energy of society.

The Connection Between Karma and Energy

There's a deep connection between karma and energy. Just as energy is associated with every substance, a specific energy is linked to every action. Our every thought, word, and deed releases a type of energy that is felt not only within us but also in the external world. This energy can be positive or negative, and its effect grows or diminishes over time.

Positive Karma and Its Energy

When we perform good and positive actions, that energy not only balances our lives but also grants us mental peace, physical health, and spiritual joy. This energy also affects those around us and creates an atmosphere of love, peace, and cooperation in society.

Negative Karma and Its Energy

Negative actions, such as lying, deceiving, or harming someone, generate negative energy. This energy also affects our mind, body, and soul. Prolonged practice of negative karma can lead to a stressful, unhappy, and unbalanced life. This energy also has a negative impact on society, increasing the likelihood of conflict, hatred, and violence.

Impact of Energy at the Place of Action

Wherever actions are performed, an accumulation of energy occurs at that place. For instance, if we repeatedly perform good deeds at a specific location, the energy of that place becomes positive. For example, in temples, gurdwaras, or any sacred site, people regularly perform worship, meditation, and good deeds, leading to an accumulation of positive energy there. The effect of this energy is felt by everyone who visits that place.

Conversely, if negative actions occur at a place, such as quarrels, crimes, or other wrongdoings, a flow of negative energy pervades that location. This energy not only affects the people living there but also negatively impacts new visitors to that place.

Understanding the Accumulation of Energy at the Place of Action

It's important to understand that karma isn't performed by an isolated individual. Wherever we live, in whatever society we reside, the karma of that place affects us too. When we live in a community, village, city, or country, the impact of that society's collective karma falls upon us. The collective energy of society is either positive or negative. If every individual in a society performs good deeds, that place fills with positive energy, benefiting everyone.

We see examples of this in some places where people collectively engage in good actions, such as cleanliness, helping others, love, and cooperation. As a result, the atmosphere of that place becomes pleasant and peaceful. Whereas if negative karma dominates a society, the environment there is filled with negativity, and its people face mental stress, anxiety, and problems.

Individual Karma and Collective Energy

Our individual actions don't just affect our own lives; they also influence the energy around us. When we reside in a place, we become part of that place's collective energy. If more positive actions occur in that place, we too become part of that positive energy, and if negative actions happen, we also feel the effect of its energy.

Impact of Positive Energy

When we steer our actions in a good and positive direction, we not only purify our individual energy but also influence the collective energy of society. This empowers us mentally and physically. The effect of this positive energy brings feelings of happiness, peace, and prosperity into our lives.

Impact of Negative Energy

When we perform negative actions, our energy becomes negative. This impact is felt not only in our lives but also by those around us. The accumulation of negative energy can increase stress, conflicts, and depression, which adversely affect our lives and society.

The Importance of Karma

Karma is important because the energy of every action we perform accumulates, and it impacts every area of life. This gives us an opportunity to understand that whatever we do shapes and directs our lives. If we move towards positive actions, we not only purify our own energy but also make the world a better place.

Accumulation of Energy

The accumulation of energy at the place of action not only affects our individual lives but also shapes the collective energy of society and the world. The impact of our actions is felt both within us and externally. When we perform good deeds, we generate positive energy that benefits not only us but also our society and nation. Conversely, negative actions not only affect our individual energy but also have an adverse impact on society. Therefore, it's essential that we direct our actions powerfully, positively, and auspiciously, so that we can create an energy that can better our lives and society.

Chapter 14. Sources of Spiritual Awakening

Friends, if you want to understand the power of karma more deeply, if you wish to know the truth about life, death, and reincarnation—then today I am suggesting some books and videos that can not only expand your knowledge but also change the direction of your life. These are the pieces of evidence and studies that will introduce you to the profound mysteries of karma, the soul, and life. In my own spiritual quest, various books and resources have helped me along the way. Here, I am sharing some names of books and videos that might also assist you in understanding the deep secrets of karma, the soul, and life.

But before you read or watch these resources, I want to tell you a story about Lord Buddha that profoundly affected me.

Once, Lord Buddha was walking towards a village with his disciples. Along the way, an inquisitive man approached him and humbly asked, "Lord, do gods truly exist?" Buddha smiled and posed a question back to him, "What do you believe?" The man replied, "I fully believe that gods exist." Hearing this, Buddha gravely said, "Your notion is wrong, gods do not exist." The man was astonished and left. After walking a little further, another man came and repeated the same question, "Do gods exist?" Buddha again asked, "What do you believe?" He replied, "I don't think there's any god anywhere." To this, Buddha said, "You are mistaken, gods do exist."

Now, seeing all this, his disciples were very surprised. They respectfully asked, "Lord, why did you give two completely opposite answers to the same question?" Then Buddha replied with profound depth, "Because both of them had merely assumed whether gods existed or not, without seeking or experiencing. My purpose is for them to put in a little effort themselves, to search, to investigate, to experience it personally—not to blindly accept."

Friends, this is what I want to tell you as well—don't just assume; rather, seek the truth with your own effort, and recognize the truth.

In this quest, the books and videos that have helped me might open new doors for you too.

Books

- **Life After Life** — Raymond Moody
- **Evidence of the Afterlife** — Jeffrey Long & Paul Perry
- **Jeevatma Jagat Ke Niyam** — Khorshed Bhavnagri
- **The Tibetan Book of the Dead**
- **Luminous Landscape of the Afterlife** (English)
- **Science of Meditation**
- **Proof of Heaven** — Dr. Eben Alexander
- **Journey of Souls** — Dr. Michael Newton
- **Many Lives, Many Masters** — Dr. Brian L. Weiss

Videos to Watch

- **Spiritual Reality (Power of Meditation)**
- **The Secret (Law of Attraction)**
- **After Death (Angel Studios Documentary)**

These books and videos teach you, through real-life events and scientific research, the importance of karma, the deep power of meditation, and the mystery of life after death.

If you truly wish to bring **peace, love, and elevation** into your life, studying these resources can be the next step in your spiritual journey.

Chapter 15. Questions and Answers

Karma is a subject that often sparks questions in our minds. Every action we take in life ultimately returns to us with its consequences. To understand karma and its results, many curiosities arise within us. Do good deeds always bring good outcomes? Do we get punished for bad deeds? Can we change our karma? In this chapter, we will delve deeper into karma through some key questions and their answers.

Chapter 1: Is Anyone Watching Our Karma?

Question: Is anyone watching our karma?

Answer: Yes, according to the book, there is an unknown power or intelligent system in the universe that records our actions, and their consequences accurately return to us.

Question: What are some examples of the universe's balance?

Answer: The balance of living beings in nature, the complex structure of the human body, the natural cycle of oxygen and carbon dioxide, the creation of life from a seed, and the precise balance of planets are examples of the universe's equilibrium.

Question: Why is karma the fundamental truth of life?

Answer: Karma is the fundamental truth of life because whatever we think, speak, and do is recorded somewhere, and its consequences return to us.

Chapter 2: Karma and Life's Precious Connection

Question: What was common among the great souls who attained ultimate knowledge?

Answer: All of them shared a deep commonality in self-reflection, meditation, and performing auspicious deeds.

Question: What is the fundamental basis of life?

Answer: The fundamental basis of life is to always keep one's actions pure, righteous, and virtuous.

Question: Why is karma not just a physical act?

Answer: Karma is not only what we do, but also what we don't do when we should have.

Question: What lesson does the Mahabharata example teach about karma?

Answer: If upholding a vow means supporting injustice, then breaking such a vow at that moment is appropriate, and dharma lies not just in rules, but in duty and justice.

Chapter 3: Unique Benefits of Right Karma

Question: How can one avoid bad karma even in difficult situations?

Answer: One can avoid bad karma by controlling one's mind, resorting to discernment and patience, and acting in a completely awakened state.

Question: What are some benefits of right actions?

Answer: Physical fitness, peace in the family, progress in work, spiritual power, destruction of past life sins, and a bright aura are some benefits of right actions.

Question: What is the connection between peace of mind and physical health?

Answer: Mental and physical health are interconnected; the burden of wrong actions puts heavy pressure on the mind, which also affects physical health and can lead to many illnesses.

Question: What is proven by Dr. Masaru Emoto's experiments?

Answer: His experiments prove that the energy of our thoughts and actions affects not only our lives but also everything around us.

Question: How does right karma affect the energy of the workplace?

Answer: If you work with honesty, hard work, and dedication at your workplace, that place feels pure, spiritually peaceful, and impactful, leading to prosperity in work and business.

Question: What are the proofs of the soul's existence?

Answer: Out-of-body experiences (OBE) for meditators and Near-Death Experiences (NDE) in hospitals are some proofs of the soul's existence.

Question: What is an aura and how do right actions affect it?

Answer: An aura is an invisible energy field around every person that reflects their emotions, thoughts, and health; performing right actions makes the aura bright and positive.

Chapter 4: Harms Caused by Wrong Karma

Question: What are some harms caused by wrong karma?

Answer: Spiritual damage, impact on physical health, disharmony in the family, strained relationships, financial loss, mental burden, and lack of positivity are some harms caused by wrong karma.

Question: How does wrong karma affect the soul?

Answer: Wrong actions bring impurity to the soul, disturb inner peace, and make us experience restlessness and dissatisfaction.

Question: What goes with us after death?

Answer: After death, our soul embarks on a journey with its karma; our actions create our "karma account" that determines the direction of the soul.

Question: What impact do wrong actions have on physical health?

Answer: Wrong actions increase stress and anxiety, which can lead to high blood pressure, heart disease, depression, and other health problems.

Question: How do wrong actions bring disharmony to the family?

Answer: Money earned through wrong deeds and family members being involved in wrong actions can disrupt happiness and peace in the home.

Question: What effect does trying to hide wrong actions have on the mind?

Answer: The process of hiding wrong actions consumes mental energy, fatigues the mind, weakens memory, and hinders mental clarity.

Question: Why is wealth earned unethically unstable and negative?

Answer: When money is earned by deceiving or harming others, their negative emotions become attached to the wealth, which can increase stress, unrest, and mental problems in life.

Chapter 5: Reincarnation and the Soul: The Cycle of Karma

Question: What is the principle of reincarnation?

Answer: The principle of reincarnation is the philosophy of life's continuous journey, in which the soul is immortal, and the cycle of birth and death is a means for the soul's progress and purification.

Question: What is the fundamental basis of reincarnation in Indian philosophy?

Answer: In Indian philosophy, the fundamental basis of reincarnation is karma; the soul receives a new life as a result of its actions.

Question: What are Akashic Records?

Answer: Akashic Records can be understood as an invisible book or energy field of life and the cosmos, in which a record of all thoughts, actions, experiences, and emotions of every soul from every birth is preserved.

Chapter 6: Karma Yoga and Types of Karma

Question: What is the meaning of Karma Yoga?

Answer: Karma Yoga teaches us that we should perform our duties selflessly, without expecting any fruit, with complete honesty and dedication.

Question: What are the three types of karma?

Answer: The three types of karma are: Sanchita Karma (sum of actions from past lives), Prarabdha Karma (portion of Sanchita Karma destined to be experienced in this life), and Kriyamana Karma (actions being performed in the present).

Question: What is the difference between karma and destiny?

Answer: Karma is the result of our own efforts, while destiny is considered predetermined; the principle of karma teaches that we can change our destiny through our actions.

Question: What are the three levels of performing karma?

Answer: The three levels of performing karma are: thinking and feeling (karma of the mind), speaking (karma of speech), and physical actions (physical form of karma).

Chapter 7: Good and Bad Karma: A Comparison

Question: How do we identify good and bad karma?

Answer: Good actions are those that bring positive change to others' lives and provide long-term benefits, while bad actions have a negative impact; the true evaluation of karma depends on the underlying intention, emotion, and its consequences.

Question: Why is true knowledge of karma essential?

Answer: True knowledge of karma gives us the power to make right decisions in life and prevents us from evaluating karma bound by societal conventions and limitations.

Chapter 8: The Path of the Observer

Question: What does it mean to become an observer (Drashta)?

Answer: Becoming an observer means seeing oneself as a witness beyond all actions and their consequences, understanding that we are merely characters in this world.

Question: What is the first step to becoming an observer?

Answer: The first step to becoming an observer is to detach oneself from the emotions of one's actions and to know that every experience is a passing moment that should only be observed.

Question: What is the biggest benefit of becoming an observer?

Answer: The biggest benefit of becoming an observer is that you experience neutrality, freeing yourself from the ego of action and the fear of consequences.

Question: What does it mean to see life merely as a witness?

Answer: It means observing life without any interference, seeing whatever is happening not from within, but from outside, as if enjoying a movie.

Chapter 9: Practicing Daily Good Karma

Question: What is a simple way to make the practice of good karma easier?

Answer: Making meditation a part of your life is a simple and effective way to make the practice of good karma easier.

Question: How does meditation purify the mind?

Answer: Meditation gradually calms the negative thoughts and wrong desires hidden within us, causing the mind's inherent purity to manifest in thoughts and actions.

Question: What does meditation connect us to?

Answer: Meditation connects us to the divine and makes us realize that we are a small but important part of this universe.

Question: Who is the greatest companion on the journey of improving karma?

Answer: Meditation is the greatest companion on the journey of improving karma.

Question: What are some ways to change bad habits?

Answer: Regular meditation practice, controlling speech, visualizing the future consequences of one's words and actions, and controlling thoughts are some ways to change bad habits.

Question: How do our actions return to us?

Answer: Whatever karma you perform, it will return to you, and likely amplified.

Chapter 10: Development of Society & Nation

Question: What is the true development of society and the nation?

Answer: True development is that which brings change within every individual, bringing purity and positivity to their thoughts and actions.

Question: Besides economic progress, what else is important for development?

Answer: True development occurs when the benefits of economic prosperity reach all sections of society and individuals bring positive change to society through their actions.

Question: What feelings do right actions promote in society?

Answer: Right actions promote feelings of trust and love in society.

Question: How can education contribute to societal development?

Answer: It is essential to include moral and social responsibilities in education so that children become better citizens and can bring about positive change in society.

Question: Who is a good leader?

Answer: A good leader is one who not only performs right actions themselves but also guides others in the right direction through their conduct.

Question: How can every individual contribute to the development of society and the nation?

Answer: Every individual can contribute through small actions, such as helping someone in need, educating children, or protecting the environment.

Chapter 11: The Importance of Karma Education in Schools

Question: Why is it necessary to impart karma education in schools?

Answer: Imparting karma education in schools is extremely necessary because it is here that children's mental and moral development takes place, and education on right actions can show them the path to living a strong and positive life.

Question: What is the objective of karma education?

Answer: The objective of karma education is to help children understand the difference between good and bad actions, develop their ability to make right decisions, make them ethical and compassionate, and make them realize their responsibilities towards society.

Question: How does karma education help in children's personality development?

Answer: When children are taught about good deeds, their personality develops in a positive direction; they understand their duties and strive to direct their actions correctly in society.

Question: What are some benefits of karma education?

Answer: Positive mindset, contribution to society, self-control, and moral responsibility are some benefits of karma education.

Question: What is the teacher's contribution to making karma education effective in schools?

Answer: The teacher's contribution is very important because they are role models for children, and children learn from their conduct how to perform true actions.

Chapter 12: The Path to Living with Peace and Love

Question: How can most of life's problems be solved?

Answer: If we learn the art of living with love and peace, most of life's problems begin to solve themselves.

Question: What is not the true reason for happiness and peace?

Answer: Simply earning money, building a big beautiful house, or getting a high-paying job is not the true reason for happiness and peace.

Question: What is the true purpose of life?

Answer: The true purpose of life is a spiritual journey, to further refine the soul and attain higher consciousness.

Question: How is meditation helpful on the path of peace and love?

Answer: Through meditation, we can raise our level of consciousness, and when consciousness rises, happiness, peace, love, and solutions will all effortlessly come into life.

Question: How should one keep one's mind towards others?

Answer: One should keep one's mind clear and pure towards everyone, forgive everyone from the heart, and have feelings of love for everyone.

Question: What is the connection between self-acceptance and peace and love?

Answer: When we truly accept ourselves and recognize the good within us, peace and love automatically enter our lives.

Chapter 13: Karmic Energy at the Place of Action

Question: What does every action we take emit?

Answer: Every action we take emits its own energy waves, which not only affect our lives but are also connected to the place, society, and world where that action is performed.

Question: How does energy accumulate at the place of action?

Answer: When we perform an action, its energy accumulates at that place, and this energy can be either positive or negative.

Question: What is the effect of positive karmic energy?

Answer: Positive karmic energy balances our lives, provides mental peace, physical health, and spiritual joy, and creates an atmosphere of love, peace, and cooperation in society.

Question: What is the effect of negative karmic energy?

Answer: Negative karmic energy affects the mind, body, and soul; prolonged negative actions can lead to a stressful, unhappy, and unbalanced life, and also have a negative impact on society.

Question: How does the collective energy of society affect us?

Answer: When we live in a society, the influence of that society's collective actions falls upon us; if more positive actions occur in society, we also become part of that positive energy.

Chapter 14: Sources of Spiritual Awakening

Question: What sources are suggested for spiritual awakening?

Answer: Some books like 'Life After Life', 'Evidence of the Afterlife', 'Jeevatma Jagat Ke Niyam', 'The Tibetan Book of the Dead', 'Proof of Heaven', 'Journey of Souls', 'Many Lives, Many Masters', and videos like 'Spiritual Reality (Power of Meditation)', 'The Secret (Law of Attraction)', 'After Death' are suggested as sources for spiritual awakening.

Question: What lesson is learned from the story of Lord Buddha?

Answer: The story of Lord Buddha teaches us that we should not simply believe something, but rather seek the truth with our own effort, recognize the truth, and experience it ourselves.

Question: What is taught in the suggested books and videos?

Answer: These sources teach the importance of karma, the power of meditation, and the mystery of life after death through real events and scientific research.

Conclusion:

The questions that arise about karma and its consequences play a significant role in understanding our lives. Karma is not merely a matter of action and result, but it is the entire philosophy of our lives. Our actions are a reflection of our thoughts, our emotions, and our inner world. When we correctly understand the answers to these questions, we can become more responsible and aware of our actions. The principle of karma not only shows us the direction to improve our lives but also inspires us for the welfare of society and the nation.

Review

Overview of Chapters: A Summary of Key Learnings

Let's briefly review the main conclusions from the chapters discussed so far.

Karma and the Cosmic Order

It's crucial to deeply understand karma and practice good deeds in life. Our actions influence the future, and we should always strive to do good. The impact of our karma extends beyond ourselves to the world. Something remains after life. The universe is balanced by an unknown, intelligent power or energy; this is no mere coincidence. The balance of nature, the complexity of the human body, natural cycles, the growth of a tree from a seed, the precise alignment of planets, and Jupiter's protection of Earth are all proofs of this. Karma is not just a theory but the fundamental truth of life that shapes our existence every moment. The fruits of karma are always received, whether in this life or the next. Our small and large actions impact present and future lives. Right actions are important, and wrong actions weaken the soul. In this world, only our karma is permanent and accompanies us after death. Every birth offers the soul an opportunity to improve, to become more compassionate and loving.

The Connection Between Karma and Life

Great enlightened beings emphasized meditation and good deeds. Karma is inherent to life; even inaction is a form of karma. Remaining silent in the face of injustice is also part of wrong karma. Dharma and public welfare are greater than any vow. Breaking a vow is justified if it serves to protect dharma. Dharma lies not in rules, but in duty and justice. This book is not based on any specific religion or deity, but on the universal truth of karma.

Benefits of Right Karma

Even in difficult situations, it's possible to avoid wrong actions; choose the right path with discernment and patience. Right actions bring mental peace, self-respect, contentment, and positive energy into life. The serenity gained from right actions is more valuable than material comforts. Right actions steer the karmic cycle in a positive direction and open doors of opportunity. Right actions elevate one's personality, strengthen the soul, and become an inspiration for others. Physical well-being, family peace, progress in work, spiritual power, eradication of past life sins, and a bright aura are benefits of right actions. Right actions lead to a calm mind, which positively affects physical health and prevents diseases. Mental and physical health are interconnected. Wrong actions bring discord and negative energy into the home. Right actions foster positive energy and love in the home. Good deeds at the workplace bring positive energy, peace, and progress. Right actions strengthen the soul and elevate it to a higher level. Evidence of the soul's existence comes from meditative experiences and NDE/OBE. Good and bad deeds are real; karma is recorded (Akashic Records). Right actions balance negative karma from past lives and eliminate negative energy. The aura is the energy field around us. Right actions make the aura bright and positive, improving health, relationships, and self-confidence. Kirlian photography and biofield research provide scientific evidence for this.

Harms Caused by Wrong Karma

Wrong actions bring impurity to the soul, disrupt inner peace, and cause restlessness. The energy of karma remains with the soul even after death and influences future births ("karma account"). Stress and anxiety from wrong actions can lead to many physical and mental illnesses. Wrong actions (immorality, lies) break trust and damage relationships, increasing loneliness and stress. Attempts to hide mistakes consume mental energy, cause irritability, and affect relationships. Scientific research (cognitive dissonance, shadow theory) also confirms this. Wealth earned through wrong means (deceit, injustice) brings negative energy, which can cause stress, unrest, and mental problems in life. Spiritual organizations and psychological research also believe that unethical wealth does not bring contentment. Great personalities like Buddha, Osho, and Vivekananda also emphasized earning pure wealth. Wrong actions generate guilt, dissatisfaction, and stress, which disrupt mental peace and weaken brain function. Efforts to hide mistakes tire the brain, weaken memory, and reduce decision-making ability. Wrong actions bring negativity into life, corrupt thinking, and adversely affect those around us.

Reincarnation, Soul, and the Karmic Cycle

The soul is immortal, and the cycle of birth and death is a means for the soul's progress and purification. The law of conservation of energy aligns with the immortality of the soul. The soul receives a new life according to its karma; this cycle continues until liberation. Buddha, Osho, and Vivekananda considered this the journey of soul development and the fruits of karma. Scientific research presents evidence of reincarnation. Cases like Shanti Devi and James Leininger are examples. Reincarnation is the path for the soul's development, purification, and attainment of higher states through right actions. Akashic Records are the universe's invisible 'book' or energy field, in which all thoughts, actions, and experiences of every soul from every birth are recorded. This is a vast database of karma that determines the direction of the next birth. Edgar Cayce, Dolores Cannon, Michael Newton, and Raymond Moody have worked on this.

Karma Yoga and Types of Karma

Karma Yoga teaches us to act selflessly, without worrying about results, with complete honesty and dedication. There are three types of karma: Sanchita Karma (sum of actions from past lives), Prarabdha Karma (portion of Sanchita Karma destined to be experienced in this life), and Kriyamana Karma (actions being performed in the present). We are responsible for our actions and can improve our future. Positive thinking, helping others, truth, non-violence, knowledge, meditation, and yoga are helpful for this. Karma is not just a physical act, but occurs at all three levels: thinking (mind), speaking (speech), and doing (body). Thoughts and emotions are the first karma. Words are also karma that have a profound impact. Physical actions are their final form. All three are interconnected.

Identifying Good and Bad Karma

Whether karma is good or bad is determined not merely by its external appearance, but by **intention, circumstances, and long-term consequences**. Giving money to a beggar might seem like a good deed, but if they misuse the money and are responsible for their own bad situation, the help could become a bad deed. Performing religious acts solely for show or praise is not true karma but a display of ego. True actions are done secretly, selflessly, and out of a sense of duty. A woman leaving an abusive husband might seem bad from a societal perspective, but for self-preservation and liberation from suffering, it is not a bad action. Intention and circumstance are crucial. Evaluate karma based on intention (pure or selfish), circumstance (context), and consequence (long-term impact).

The Path of the Observer

Good actions can bring ego, and bad actions can bring guilt. The path of the observer transcends both. To become an observer means to see oneself as a witness, detached from action and its consequences. To view every experience as a passing moment. Not to judge karma as right/wrong. The observer state brings neutrality – freedom from the ego of action and the fear of consequences. Karma becomes a natural flow, not a burden. Practice: sit calmly and observe thoughts, emotions, and actions without judgment. Observe karma passively. Meditate. Benefits: This path purifies the soul, frees it from the cycle of karma, and helps in self-realization.

Practicing Good Karma in Daily Life

If improving karma seems difficult, meditation is the most effective solution. Meditation calms negative thoughts and desires, purifies the mind, and brings positivity. It reduces the desire for wrong actions and increases awareness. Improving karma is a journey that requires patience and determination. Failures may occur, but keep striving. Methods of practice: regular meditation, control over speech (speak thoughtfully), visualization of the future (imagine the effects of actions), and control over thoughts (positive thinking, freedom from deceit and fraud) are essential. Every action returns to us, possibly amplified. Good deeds bring happiness and peace; bad deeds bring suffering. Practice brings miraculous changes in life.

Karma in Social and National Development

The true development of society/nation is not just economic progress, but a change within citizens, purity in their thoughts and actions. True progress is based on the moral values and right actions of citizens. Right actions promote trust, love, and positive energy in society, reducing crime and inequality. Karma education makes children responsible citizens and gives them the ability to make right decisions. Incorporating it into the curriculum, using dialogue and stories, is helpful.

The Path of Peace and Love

Living with peace and love is more important than material comforts. The true purpose of life is a spiritual journey and purifying the soul. Meditation raises the level of consciousness, bringing peace, love, and solutions effortlessly into life. Learning from others: learn what not to do in life from conflicted families. Forgiveness and purity: keep the mind clear, forgive everyone, have feelings of love – this is the nature of the soul and the path to peace. Empathy, understanding, and self-acceptance are also necessary.

Karmic Energy and Location

Every action emits energy waves that affect the place, society, and world. This energy can be positive or negative. Energy accumulates at the place of action. Good deeds make a place positive (like a temple), bad deeds make it negative (crime scene). The collective actions of society affect us. Our individual actions also influence collective energy.

Sources of Spiritual Awakening

To understand the power of karma, and the truth of life,

death, and rebirth, some important books and videos can be helpful. These include 'Life After Life', 'Evidence of the Afterlife', 'Jeevatma Jagat Ke Niyam', 'The Tibetan Book of the Dead', 'Luminous Landscape of the Afterlife', 'Science of Meditation', 'Proof of Heaven', 'Journey of Souls', 'Many Lives, Many Masters', 'Spiritual Reality (Power of Meditation)', 'The Secret (Law of Attraction)', and 'After Death (Angel Studios Documentary)'.

Conclusion: A New Beginning

The questions that arise about karma and its consequences play a crucial role in understanding our lives. Karma isn't just a matter of action and result; it's the entire philosophy of our existence. Our actions are a reflection of our thoughts, our emotions, and our inner world. When we truly understand the answers to these questions, we can become more responsible and aware of our actions. The principle of karma not only guides us towards improving our own lives but also inspires us for the betterment of society and the nation.

Everyone in the world will read this book, and through its influence, this world will become as beautiful as heaven, where everyone will find immense joy in living.

The Book is Complete and a New Life is Begins...

www.ingramcontent.com/pod-product-compliance
Ingram Content Group UK Ltd.
Pitfield, Milton Keynes, MK11 3LW, UK
UKHW021409190726
13845UKWH00028B/970

9 789334 306385